REVELATION AND REASON IN ISLAM

A.J. ARBERRY

Qadeem Press

Qadeem Press

Qadeem Press Edition
Breathing Life into Forgotten Pages
www.qadeempress.com

Originally Published by George Allen & Unwin Ltd in 1957
Reprinted by Qadeem Press in 2025

CONTENTS

I

THE problem of the relationship between revelation and reason is indeed one of the most famous and profound topics in the history of human thought. It is a topic which, though debated without intermission now for some two thousand years, appears not to lose anything of its fascination and freshness, for all the dust overspreading the countless volumes of dead, or seemingly dead metaphysics and theology. In choosing as my theme for this course of lectures 'Revelation and Reason in Islam' I am all too conscious of the slightness of the contribution to that long debate which it will fall to me to make, in so short a time and upon the basis of knowledge so limited. If it were possible to institute a full review of this sublime dilemma as it affected and was affected by the Mohammedan faith, that would undoubtedly take us some considerable distance towards understanding and stating the problem as a whole. The problem as a whole has never yet, so far as I am aware, been anywhere stated; and until the whole problem has been correctly stated, it is obviously vain to look for anything approaching a satisfactory solution, assuming that a satisfactory solution is in any case discoverable. It should not be necessary to stress, what is so apparent as to be a truism, that the true nature of the conflict or concord between reason and revelation will not be seized by those who confine their curiosity to its manifestation in Christianity alone, or in Judaism alone, or in Islam alone. Each system of beliefs resting upon faith in a Divine revelation introduces its own distinctive set of variations; all these variations need to be studied if the theme itself is to be appreciated in all its fecund richness. In these lectures it is proposed merely to call attention to a few aspects of the problem as it happened in Islam. It would be improper to close these introductory sentences without proclaiming my indebtedness to the work of those other scholars who have laboured in this field, far longer and more fruitfully than I have done. In particular I would mention J. W. Sweetman, whose *Islam and Christian Theology* will when complete serve many years to come as the authoritative guide to future researchers; and Louis Gardet, writer of many books and articles of first importance for the study that is our present concern and especially, with Father M. M. Anawati, author of that admirably erudite monograph *Introduction à la théologie musulmane.*[1]

'Wherever and whenever the problem of the relations of faith and reason may happen to be asked, the abstract conditions of its solution are bound to remain the same.'[2] E. Gilson's acute observation makes an excellent point of departure, though the words *abstract conditions* are to be emphasised and perhaps discussed; that however is a task for a psychologist rather than an orientalist. The beginning of this story, at all events in the west, is with the Greeks. Plato, who was pre-eminently a political philosopher, found it necessary to assume the existence of a divine lawgiver, in order to furnish with authority the ordinances by which he hoped to establish his ideal state. 'No one,' says the Athenian Stranger, 'who in obedience to the laws believed that there were Gods, ever intentionally did any unholy act, or uttered any unlawful word';[3] and he added, how poignantly, 'Who can be calm when he is called upon to prove the existence of the Gods?'[4] For 'men say that we ought not to inquire into the supreme God and the nature of the universe, nor busy ourselves in searching out the causes of things, and that such inquiries are impious; whereas the very opposite is the truth.'[5] That goes to the very heart of the quarrel between faith and intellect. So in the *Timaeus* Plato worked out his celebrated theory of God and creation. When Aristotle in his turn felt obliged to extend the range of physics and metaphysics to demonstrate the logical necessity of an unmoved mover,[6] he was giving scientific form to the emotional argument that 'the world is the fairest of creations, and He is the best of causes.'[7] And when he came to consider what manner of being that First Cause might be, he reached the momentous conclusion, to which his ethical thinking inevitably led him, that 'the activity of God, which surpasses all others in blessedness, must be contemplative; and of human activities, therefore, that which is most akin to this must be most of the nature of happiness.'[8]

'Plato's Greece was the source of the tradition according to which the existence of God requires and admits of proof by argument.'[9] That is the beginning—in the west—of the mind's quest for its Maker. 'None of the Old Testament writers treats of the existence of deity as if it were an open question or in any sense problematic.'[10] For the soul of the Semites found God in revelation; and 'what we have said about the Old Testament applies to the New with little variation.'[11] But then began the great and immensely stimulating encounter between Greece and Israel. Philo was the first influential thinker who 'started with the twin conceptions that Scripture was a divine revelation and that Greek philosophy was true,' and who consequently found himself faced by the problem of effecting 'the reconciliation of philosophy with the Law, Plato with Moses.'[12] The devices of allegory to which he was obliged to resort have many parallels in the writings of later Christian and Moslem speculators. Men like Clement and Origen carried over with them into Christianity ideas they had acquired during their earlier training in the schools of Greek philosophy, so that at times 'the Church appears as the insurance society for the ideas of Plato and Zeno.'[13] The theosophy and mysticism of the Neoplatonists increasingly dominated Christian thought, paving the way for their triumph in Islam. This invasion by reason of the sacred territory of revelation naturally did not take place without violent protest. What the Christian fundamentalist Tertullian said in the third century is a pre-echo of the voice of the Moslem Ibn Taimīya in the thirteenth: 'Heresies are themselves instigated by philosophy. The same subject matter is discussed over and over again by the heretics and the philosophers; the same arguments are involved. . . .' Unhappy Aristotle! who invented for these men dialectics, the art of building up and pulling down, an art so far-fetched in its conjectures, so harsh in its arguments, so productive of contentions—embarrassing even to itself, retracting everything, and really treating of nothing. . . . Away with all attempts to produce a mottled Christianity of Stoic, Platonic and dialectic composition! We want no curious disputation after possessing Christ Jesus, no inquisition after enjoying the Gospel! With our faith, we desire no further belief.'[14] St. Anselm's *non in dialectica complacuit deo salvum facere populum suum* would have commanded the hearty assent of many followers of Aḥmad ibn Ḥanbal.

The Christian debate between revelation and reason, all the louder for having silenced the last mutterings of Hellenistic paganism, still raged in Alexandria and Antioch when a prophet was born in Mecca, whose followers were within a century to be masters of the old intellectual centres of the Near East. The scene was thus set for a renewal of the old argument, with revelation however not now the verities of the Bible but of the Koran. Reason for its part relied upon the identical armoury of Greek philosophy and science, made accessible to Moslem controversialists thanks mainly to the labours of Christian translators; to that powerful panoply the Arabs needed to add virtually no new weapons. Our task is to consider, within the narrow limits already advertised, how the conflict developed in its new setting.

'The Muslim idea of revelation gathers it up in a book, the Christian in a Person.'[15] H. M. Gwatkin's acute observation is elaborated in the fuller statement of William Temple: 'In Islam a claim is made for a revelation in the Koran similar at first sight to that found in the Bible, and Mohammed is regarded by his followers with a veneration greater than that paid by Jews or Christians to any prophet. But he is still the Prophet and no more; the revelation is in his message, not in himself; it is therefore still only on the subjective side of the subject-object relation. Moreover it mainly consists of precepts and the requirement is of obedience to a law rather than of loyalty and love to a Person.'[16] Fundamentally that is a correct statement of the position; the Koran, accepted as the eternal Word of God, contains the whole of God's final revelation to man;[17] Mohammed was nothing more than a human being.[18] The message he received was found to be a sufficient guide to his followers in those early heroic days of a militant and expanding faith, when 'Islam . . . meant the old Hebrew battle-cry, Let God arise, and let his enemies be scattered.'[19] On the battlefield of Siffin, when the first great conflict in Islam awaited decision, it was the Koran that was raised on the lances of Mu'āwiya's soldiers, and 'Alī accepted that as a wholly valid arbitrament. But it did not take long for the discovery to be made that the Koran by itself did not hold the solution of all problems; the meaning of the sacred text was by no means always clear, for all that it described itself over and over again as a 'manifest Book';[20] and provision had unfortunately not been made for all contingencies. The acts and sayings of Mohammed were therefore eagerly canvassed from those of his immediate disciples still surviving, and these were by common consent accorded an authority no less binding than that of the Koran. In this sense therefore it is not quite accurate to say that the Koran is the only revelation accepted by Islam; the inspired life and utterances of the Prophet were recognised by all Moslem opinion as furnishing a useful and binding supplement, particularly when it came to grappling with the claims of reason.

It has been said by A. J. Wensinck that 'the debates on predestination inaugurated rationalism in Islam.'[21] In the theological arena certainly the first momentous contest to be fought was that between the Qadarīya, who championed man's free will, and the Jabarīya who held all human acts to be predestined.[22] But Islam had been from its origins as much a political as a religious movement, or rather it has seen no division between religion and politics, and it could therefore be argued that the first rational act in its history was the recognition of Abū Bakr as Mohammed's caliph. The acceptance of reason as an ally of faith in any case goes back further still; that is the repeated declaration of the Koran:[23]

> Surely in the creation of the heavens and earth
> and in the alternation of night and day
> there are signs for men possessed of minds.

In the decade before the last war Christian theologians made much of 'the growing tendency to substitute for the old distinction of natural and revealed knowledge of God the new distinction between a general and a special revelation.'[24] Some writers indeed added a third category: 'This divine self-communication takes place in a *general* way, we believe, in the whole order of nature and the whole process of history; in a *special* way in the history of the 'chosen people' and its spiritual offspring, the Christian Church; in a *unique* way in Jesus Christ.'[25] This idea, stimulating and fruitful as it seemed at the time, now appears to be little more than a reformulation of a principle implicitly accepted for many centuries. So far as Islam is concerned, the doctrine of a general and a special revelation is fully justified by reference to the Koran. *The heavens declare the glory of God; and the firmament showeth his handywork*[26] is an ever-repeated theme:[27]

> And of His signs
> is that He created you of dust; then lo,
> you are mortals, all scattered abroad.
> And of His signs

is that He created for you, of yourselves,
spouses, that you might repose in them,
and He has set between you love and mercy.
Surely in that are signs for a people who consider.
And of His signs
is the creation of the heavens and earth
and the variety of your tongues and hues.
Surely in that are signs for all living beings.
And of His signs
is your slumbering by night and day,
and your seeking after His bounty.
Surely in that are signs for a people who hear.
And of His signs
He shows you lightning, for fear and hope,
and that He sends down out of heaven water
and He revives the earth after it is dead.
Surely in that are signs for a people who understand.
And of His signs
is that the heaven and earth stand firm
by His command; then, when He calls you
once and suddenly, out of the earth, lo
you shall come forth.

So much for the 'whole order of nature'; as for the 'whole process of history':[28]

Is it not a guidance to them, how many
generations We destroyed before them
in whose dwelling-places they walk?
Surely in that are signs for men
possessing reason.

That is the *general* revelation; the *special* revelation is summed up in such words as:[29]

We have revealed to thee as We revealed
to Noah, and the Prophets after him,
and We revealed to Abraham, Ishmael,
Isaac, Jacob, and the Tribes,

Jesus and Job, Jonah and Aaron
and Solomon, and We gave to David
Psalms,
and Messengers We have already told thee of
before, and Messengers We have not told thee of;
and unto Moses God spoke directly—
Messengers bearing good tidings, and warning,
so that mankind might have no argument
against God, after the Messengers; God is
All-mighty, All-wise.
But God bears witness to that He has sent down
to thee; He has sent it down with His knowledge;
and the angels also bear witness; and God suffices
for a witness.

We are irresistibly put in mind of those sublime words *God, who at sundry times and in divers manners spake in time past unto the fathers by the prophets, hath in these last days spoken unto us by his Son.*[30]

The reiterated and unambiguous teaching of the Koran on the two orders of revelation—God's power as seen in His creation, and God's will as disclosed to His Messengers—opened the way to a rational discussion of religious truths long before the rise of theological controversy. Indeed in respect to some particular matters debated in Mohammed's own time, such especially as the doctrine of the resurrection, the Koran itself laid down the method of argument.[31]

Nay, but they marvel that a warner has come to
them from among them; and the unbelievers say,
'This is a marvellous thing!
What, when we are dead and become dust? That
is a far returning!'
We know what the earth diminishes of them;
with Us is a book recording.
Nay, but they cried lies to the truth
when it came to them, and so they are
in a case confused.

What, have they not beheld heaven above them,
how We have built it, and decked it out fair,
and it has no cracks?
And the earth—We stretched it forth, and cast on it
firm mountains,
and We caused to grow therein of every joyous kind
for an insight
and a reminder to every penitent servant.
And We sent down out of heaven
water blessed,
and caused to grow thereby gardens
and grain of harvest
and tall palm-trees with spathes compact,
a provision for the servants,
and thereby We revived a land that was dead.
Even so is the coming forth.

Even the varieties of response to the different categories of opponents are prescribed, or seemingly foreshadowed, in a passage which later controversialists never wearied of quoting:[32]

Call thou to the way of thy Lord
with wisdom and good admonition,
and dispute with them
in the better way.

When the Koranic term *ḥikma* (wisdom) came to be used loosely to signify philosophy, this text fortified the philosophers in their contest with the obscurantists. The verbal noun derived from *jādalhum* ('dispute with them') was to acquire the technical meaning of 'reasoned debate.' As for *mau'iẓa* ('admonition'), that was the chosen method of the preachers. This verse would be taken to confirm Aristotle's threefold differentiation of proof into demonstrative, rhetorical and dialectical.[33]

Interpretation of the Koran as a device for extending the area of its infallible authority depended in the first instance upon those elucidations by the Prophet which the faithful were able to remember or, if need be, invent. Straightforward exegesis (*tafsīr*) of the sacred text was presently allowed to the reliably informed; then to grammarians and philologists; and finally to theologians, whose annotations reflected their scholastic activities.[34] A particular variety of commentary was also provided in due course by the Sufis, who sought to justify their mystical ideas or to validate their ecstatic experiences by reference to God's Word.[35] Nor did the philosophers neglect this powerful weapon in their struggle for the mind of Islam; thus among Avicenna's more curious exercises in virtuosity are to be found Neoplatonic expositions of the emanationist theory of creation cast in the form of Koranic commentary.[36]

This last type of exegesis however belongs more properly to what was called *ta'wīl*. In the early days of Islam *tafsīr* and *ta'wīl* were regarded as more or less synonymous terms; later, *ta'wīl* was used to designate 'esoteric' as opposed to 'exoteric' interpretation.[37] The proof-text always cited in justification of *ta'wīl* is Koran III 5:

> It is He who sent down upon thee the Book,
> wherein are verses clear that are the Essence
> of the Book, and others ambiguous.
> As for those in whose hearts is swerving,
> they follow the ambiguous part, desiring
> dissension, and desiring its interpretation;
> and none knows its interpretation, save
> only God. And those firmly rooted in
> knowledge say, 'We believe in it; all
> is from our Lord'; yet none remembers, but men
> possessed of minds.

The word translated by 'interpretation' is *ta'wīl*. A

crucial point in the dispute between the professors of *ta'wīl* and their antagonists was the method of construing this famous verse. The version just given expresses the orthodox Sunnī view, whereas the Shī'ites and the philosophers took it otherwise:

> and none knows its interpretation, save only God, and those firmly rooted in knowledge; they say, 'We believe in it; all is from our Lord'. . .

Naturally it remained to determine who were qualified to be described as 'those firmly rooted in knowledge.' The identification followed unsurprising lines. The Shī'ites said that the persons meant were their Imams, who possessed a secret exegesis handed down from the Prophet's cousin and son-in-law 'Alī;[38] the philosophers claimed that the reference was to themselves.[39]

The acrimonious quarrels between the early theologians of Islam, that culminated in the sustained and bitter warfare between the Mu'tazilites and the Ahl al-Sunna, deservedly command the prior attention of scholars interested to trace how the conflict between revelation and reason broke out and developed among Mohammed's followers. Due recognition has been paid to the Christian background to these controversies,[40] and to the part played by Greek philosophy, introduced into Moslem studies, in sharpening the weapons of polemic.[41] But let it be recalled again that Islam is more than a system of religious dogmas; law always disputed with theology for primacy among the Islamic sciences,[42] and had equal need of the assistance of philosophical method. The admission of *qiyās* (analogy) as a legitimate instrument of jurisprudence, first explicitly justified by al-Shāfi'ī (d. 204/820)[43] but implicit already in the systems of Abū Ḥanīfa (d. 150/767) and Mālik ibn Anas (d. 179/795),[44] could not have happened without some awareness of the methods of Aristotelian logic. Though the derivation of *qiyās* as a legal term from the Hebrew *hiqqish* has been generally accepted,[45] it is not irrelevant to recall that this very word was chosen to translate the title of the *Analytica Priora*, while *burhān* (demonstration) was used as the equivalent of *Analytica Posteriora*.[46] In any case the debt of early Moslem jurisprudence to Greek logic and Roman law has been persuasively proved.[47] The Persian polygraph Ibn al-Muqaffa' (d. *ca.* 140/757), who is said to have translated Aristotle's logical writings from Pahlavi into Arabic,[48] thus, if the statement is true, anticipating by a considerable while those translators who made their versions directly out of the Greek,[49] in a tract that includes strictures against the ancient schools of Moslem law makes the statement that reason (*'aql*) and personal opinion (*ra'y*) have a necessary if restricted function in religion; in expressing this view he was addressing the caliph al-Mansūr.[50] When Aḥmad ibn Ḥanbal (d. 241/855), proposing to revert to the 'original Islam' in opposition to what he condemned as the rationalising excesses of the Mu'tazilites, rejected *qiyās* as an unwarranted innovation, he found himself obliged by way of compensation to extend the confines of Divine and apostolic authority by gathering together an unprecedentedly large volume of traditional sayings of the Prophet, admitting many that were excluded as of doubtful authenticity by more fastidious collectors.[51] His example, with others of a like kind, encourages the observation that extremist advocates of revelation against reason can only succeed in their manoeuvre either by enlarging the sum-total of revelation, or by claiming as revelation what others prefer to regard as the ordinary processes of reason. Even the Ḥanbalites however were unable finally to banish the analogical method from their textbooks, and that arch-enemy of the philosophers Ibn Taimīya (d. 728/1328) displays in his polemical broadsides a superb mastery of the methods of dialectical reasoning.[52]

In attempting even the briefest and most cursory review of the collision in Islam between revelation and reason, to omit all reference to the Mu'tazilite heresy would be as grotesque as to present *Hamlet* without the Prince of Denmark. But so many excellent studies of that movement have appeared in modern times, since Steiner[53] and Von Kremer[54] romantically sought to represent the champions of 'Justice and the Divine Unity' as bold free-thinkers and liberal theologians bravely battling against an engulfing tide of fanatical fundamentalism, that it would be superfluous to treat the topic at any length here.[55] We have been reminded many times that it was the Mu'tazilites who introduced the Inquisition (*miḥna*) into Islam; the saintly Aḥmad ibn Ḥanbal himself felt the lash of their fury.[56] 'It is true that a little philosophy inclineth man's mind to atheism';[57] it seems equally true that much philosophy applied to the elucidation of an infallible dogma generates great intolerance. After all that has been written about the men who made the Mu'tazila supreme for a time in Islam, and the ideas they vigorously reasoned and tyrannically imposed, it still remains attractive to speculate on the political and psychological factors involved in that vast upheaval. Faced on the one side by the rigid pietism of old-fashioned traditionists, who hated the newly-imported Greek learning and raised the battle-cry, in season and out of season, of 'Back to the Koran and the Prophet'; on the other side confronted by the fantastically wild speculations of Shī'ite extremists, some of whom went so far as to identify 'Alī with God; between whiles battling against the trinitarian Christians and the dualist Manicheans, whose insidious propaganda struck at the very roots of the monotheistic faith; in this perilous situation the Mu'tazilites might well think that the one hope of securing a strong and united Islam lay in formulating a set of doctrines acceptable to disciplined reason and maintainable by physical force. Emerging triumphant out of many passionate encounters, thanks to the sharp sword of dialectical reasoning their non-Moslem opponents had taught them to wield, they might have been excused, being human and theologians, for surrendering to an overweening and fatal arrogance. But the day of reckoning dawned in due course. When Abu 'l-Ḥasan al-Ash'arī (d. 324/935) deserted from their ranks at the height of his intellectual powers and declared himself a devoted follower of Aḥmad ibn Ḥanbal,[58] the cause of old orthodoxy gained a champion who was to assail its adversaries with their favourite weapon and to rout them from the field. The overthrow was final and complete; thenceforward the victorious Sunnīs could persecute and exterminate their erstwhile torturers at their pleasure.

The nature of God inevitably furnished the combatants with their principal point of difference; though a sufficiency of subsidiary issued availed to keep the battle, while it lasted, from ever flagging. Revelation as presented in the Koran has endowed the Creator with a wide variety of attributes that included, in addition to the metaphysical qualities of omnipotence and omniscience and the moral virtues of justice and compassion, more concrete features in the shape of hands, eyes and a face:[59]

> The Jews have said, 'God's hand is fettered.'
> Fettered are their hands, and they are cursed
> for what they have said. Nay, but His hands
> are outspread; He expends how He will.

Again, in a version of the story of Noah:[60]

> Make thou the Ark under Our eyes,
> and as We reveal.

And again:[61]

> To God belong the East and the West;
> whithersoever you turn, there is the Face of God.

God also possesses a mighty throne, on which He seated Himself after the labours of creation had been completed:[62]

> Surely your Lord is God, who created
> the heavens and the earth in six days,
> then sat Himself upon the Throne,
> directing the affair.

From earliest Islam there had been a strong preference, understandable in a people newly won from animism, to take these descriptions literally. 'It was said that God, when he grows angry, grows heavier and the throne groans under his weight like a camel saddle. Others explained that it was the throne which grew heavier, not God. Opinion was divided whether eight angels or eight kinds of angels carried the throne.'[63] The followers of Ibn Karrâm (d. 255/869) are said to have debated 'as to whether Allah is as big as His throne, whether it is equal to His breadth, and the crude statement that He is no larger than His throne on the side where He touches it, and no part of Him overlaps it.'[64] One of the leading anthropomorphists, Hishâm ibn al-Ḥakam (d. *ca.* 200/816), is credited with having stated that God 'has a body, defined, broad, high and long, of equal dimensions, radiating with light, of a fixed measure in three dimensions, in a place beyond place, like a bar of pure metal, shining as a round pearl on all sides, provided with colour, taste, smell and touch.'[65] Christianity, like Judaism, had been faced by the same kind of dilemma when confronted by the very materialistic pictures of God occurring in the Bible. St. John of Damascus (d. *ca.* 748), who as a young man 'was the boon companion of Mu'âwiyah's son Yazîd and later followed his father into that most important office in the Arab government',[66] namely the financial administratorship of Damascus, assigned a chapter of his *De Fide Orthodoxa* ('Concerning what is affirmed about God as though He had body') to a discussion of this problem. His solution might equally well have been written by a Mu'tazilite: 'All the statements concerning God, that imply body, are symbols, but have a higher meaning: for the Deity is simple and formless. Hence by God's eyes and eyelids and sight we are to understand His power of overseeing all things and His knowledge, that nothing can escape. . . . And God's countenance is the demonstration and manifestation of Himself through His works, for our manifestation is through the countenance. And God's hands mean the effectual nature of His energy, for it is with our own hands that we accomplish our most useful and valuable work.'[67]

Certainly Aḥmad ibn Ḥanbal would not have gone so far in his literalism as a certain Mughīra ibn Sa'īd al-'Ijlī, who declared that 'the limbs of Allah were formed in the shape of the letters of the alphabet, the *alif* being His leg, the '*ayn* His eye and the *hā'* another organ.'[68] But in his enunciation of the famous *bilā kaifa* formula he invented a device that may be regarded in its way as a classical resolution of the conflict between reason and revelation. 'Conscious of the dangers to the right as well as to the left, he taught that Kuran and *sunna* must be taken in their literal sense, without asking questions. . . . This rule should be applied to the anthropomorphic expressions in the Kuran, such as the face of Allah, His eyes and hands, His sitting on His throne, and His being seen by the Faithful in Paradise.'[69] This attitude, recognising the limitations of human reason, after its endorsement by al-Ash'arī became the accepted view of orthodox Islam; though not all would approve the action of Ibn Taimīya, of whom it is said that 'he said one day from the pulpit in the mosque of Damascus, "God comes down from heaven to earth, just as I am coming down now," and he came down one of the steps of the pulpit staircase.'[70]

The great al-Ash'arī summed up his picture of God in these propositions: 'We confess that God is firmly seated on His Throne. . . . We confess that God has two hands, without asking how. . . . We confess that God has two eyes, without asking how. . . . We confess that God has a face. . . . We confirm that God has a knowledge. . . . We affirm hearing and sight, and do not deny that, as do the Mu'tazila, the Jahmiyya, and the Khawārij. . . . We affirm that God has a power. . . .'[71] Contrast with this positivism the *via negativa* of the Mu'tazila: 'He is no body, nor object, nor volume, nor form, nor flesh, nor blood, nor person, nor substance, nor *accidens*, nor provided with colour, taste, smell, touch, heat, cold, moistness, dryness, length, breadth, depth, union, distinction, movement, rest or partition. Neither is He provided with parts, divisions, limbs, members, with directions, with right or left hand, before or behind, above or beneath . . . He cannot be described by any description which can be applied to creatures, in so far as they are created, neither can it be said that He is finite. . . . The senses do not reach Him, nor can man describe Him by any analogy. . . . Eyes do not see Him, sight does not reach Him, phantasy cannot conceive Him nor can He be heard by ears. He is a being, but is not as other beings. . . . Neither joy nor pleasure can reach Him, nor is He moved by hurt or pain.'[72] At least Aristotle, as we have recalled, had allowed his God a contemplative activity, 'and of human activities, therefore, that which is most akin to this must be most of the nature of happiness.'[73] It is not so surprising that the ordinary Moslem, confronted by the overwhelming and numinous portrait of the Creator that he met in his reading of the Koran, should have been tempted to suppose that the Mu'tazilites, whose metaphysics soared far beyond his comprehension, were pausing after the *lā ilāha* of the declaration of faith.

The issue on which the Mu'tazilites finally suffered irreparable defeat was their notorious doctrine that the Koran was not eternal but created. It has been well observed that their thesis in this regard 'was only a logical consequence of their denying eternal qualities [to God] as well as of their denying the eternal decree.'[74] For 'the Hellenistic school, with its more developed philosophical training, regarded the orthodox doctrine of the Attributes of God. . . . as endangering, if not actually contradicting His Unity. Here again the argument became centred on one point, the Speech of God, and since the Koran is the Speech of God in one sense, it took the (at first sight) strange theological form of affirming on the orthodox side, and denying on the other, that the Koran was uncreated and eternal, with the still more curious result that the opponents of Hellenistic philosophy reaffirmed without realising it the Hellenistic doctrine of the Logos.'[75] (It may be interjected, though not in this place debated, that the common tendency to see in the orthodox view of the Koran a Moslem version of the Logos doctrine[76] is not free from confusion.) Though rationalistic argument was advanced by both sides to support their respective positions, what was at stake was far more than the formulation of an intellectually acceptable theory. If the Koran were allowed to be created, the danger was great that it might next be alleged by those steeped in Neoplatonist thought that God's Word as revealed to Mohammed through the mediation of the archangel Gabriel shared with all created things the imperfection arising from their association with matter. The 'incomparable miracle' of the Koran must be maintained at all costs,[77] if Revelation was not to capitulate to Reason in its very stronghold.

The Koran itself provides no clear lead to those anxious to prove its eternity, for all the ingenious interpretations of[78]

> Nay, but it is a glorious Koran,
> in a guarded tablet.

The best that al-Ash'arī for his part could do by way of enlisting scriptural authority was to quote Koran XVI 42:

> The only words We say to a thing, when We
> desire it, is that We say to it, 'Be,'
> and it is.

Upon the thread of that slender text he hangs a wonderfully ingenious scholastic argument. 'If the Qur'ān had been created, God would have said to it "Be!" But the Qur'ān in His speech, and it is impossible that His speech should be spoken to. For this would necessitate a second speech, and we should have to say of this second speech and its relation to a third speech what we say of the first speech and its relation to a second speech. But this would necessitate speeches without end—which is false. And if this be false, it is false that the Qur'ān is created.'[79] Where the revealed book failed, the man to whom the revelation was made proved to have been more forthcoming, at all events to those who were prepared to be not too scrupulous in their acceptance of doubtful reports. Whereas 'canonical Tradition does not contain any trace of the debates on the Kuran and the speech of Allah,'[80] there was in circulation at least as early as the beginning of the ninth century a *ḥadīth* running as follows: 'The Koran is the speech of God. It is neither creator nor created. Whoever asserts otherwise is an unbeliever.' One variation cites the Prophet as saying, 'Everything in the heavens and earth and what between them lies is created, except God and the Koran. That is because it is His speech; from Him it originated and to Him it will return.'[81]

In a recently discovered anti-Mu'tazilite tract written by the Ḥanbalī scholar Ḍiyā' al-Dīn al-Maqdisī (569-643/1174–1245) about the year 630/1232 several different versions are given of the manner in which this saying obtained currency; in none is it claimed to rest on the Prophet's authority.[82] One report puts it into 'Alī's mouth; another assigns it to 'Abd Allāh ibn 'Abbās (d. *ca.* 70/689); while a third gives the most generally credited information[83] that 'Amr ibn Dīnār al-Makkī (d. 125/742 or 126/743) said, 'I have found our shaikhs since the last seventy years saying, "The Koran is the speech of God; from Him it originated and to Him it will return." ' This pronouncement gave rise to a curious extension of the doctrine of the eternity of the Koran. The mystery of how the divine revelation descended all at once to Mohammed was thought to be attested by Koran XLIV 2:

By the Clear Book.
We have sent it down in a blessed night.

This verse was compared with Koran XVII 88:

> If We willed, We could take away that
> We have revealed to thee.

By a neat parallelism, characteristic of Arab thought, the Prophet is alleged to have said—and Ibn Māja (d. 273/886) alone of the canonical traditionists admitted the *ḥadīth* into his corpus—'God's Book shall be come upon one night, and in the morning the people shall find that not a verse of it is left, either in the earth or in the heart of any Moslem.'[84] The circumstances that are to attend this remarkable catastrophe are described in a prophecy ascribed to 'Abd Allāh ibn Mas'ūd (d. 32/853 or 33/854): 'A red wind shall come upon the people by night from the direction of Syria, and not a verse shall remain either in the *maṣḥaf* of any man or in his heart.'

Once it had been established that the Koran was God's speech and uncreated there still remained to be determined whether the copies of the Koran in men's hands, and its pronunciation upon men's lips, were also eternal. Moslem theology did not neglect any point that could be thought of as arising, however small or unlikely it might appear. The Ḥanbalites naturally adopted an extreme attitude. Not only were the words and sounds of the Koran eternal, so that even its recital was uncreated,[85] but its parchment and binding shared these same qualitites.[86] Ibn Taimīya explained the enigma by arguing that it was not correct to assume that God's speech, by issuing from God, departed out of His Essence and dwelt in another; when the Koran is recited, the voice is that of the reciter but the speech is God's.[87] In the so-called *Testament of Abū Ḥanīfa*, which Wensinck has assigned to the first half of the ninth century,[88] a more moderate view is expressed: 'We confess that the Kuran is the speech of Allah, uncreated, His inspiration and revelation, not He, yet not other than He, but His real quality, written in the copies, recited by the tongues, preserved in the breasts, yet not residing there. The ink, the paper, the writing are created, for they are the work of men. The speech of Allah on the other hand is uncreated, for the writing and the letters and the words and the verses are manifestations of the Kuran for the sake of human needs. The speech of Allah on the other hand is self-existing, and its meaning is understood by means of these things.'[89] The creed called *al-Fiqh al-akbar*(II) which appears to belong to the tenth century[90] puts what came to be the majority standpoint of orthodox Islam quite clearly and concisely: 'Our pronouncing, writing and reciting the Kuran is created, whereas the Kuran itself is uncreated.'[91]

By the time that paragraph was formulated the battle between theologian and theologian was as good as over, though the exercise of shadow-boxing with the ancient heresies has continued down to the present day. The gulf between Sunnī and Shī'ite would never be bridged. But orthodoxy, having resolved its internal conflicts, was now free to engage philosophy proper. That contest occupied the acutest minds of Islam for the next three hundred years; the protagonists bore such famous names as Avicenna, Algazel, Avempace, Averroes; the closely-reasoned pages of the *Incoherence* and the *Incoherence of the Incoherence* fluttered on the lances of the opposing ranks. Meanwhile a third challenger for the mind and soul of Islam had entered the lists, little noticed at the beginning but destined in the end to effect a broad reconciliation between the original adversaries; so that finally a state of peace spread over the heresy-torn world of Mohammed's followers, a peace broken only by the petulant bickerings of the unassimilables. This irenic third party was the Sufi movement.

For men would not be satisfied forever with only two alternatives to choose between—belief in God either by blind and uncomprehending acceptance of what He had spoken in the Koran, or as some infinitely remote and unsubstantial fly caught in a fine-spun web of syllogistic reasoning. In every religion, however irrational or intellectualised its original appeal may be, the time comes when the human soul yearns for a personal knowledge of its Creator. 'A God perfectly comprehended would not be the God of experience, but a God who was utterly incomprehensible could not be the object of trust and love.'[92] God as revealed to Mohammed seems at first sight to be uncompromisingly transcendent; 'the prevailing feature of Allah in the Kuran is His absoluteness, His doing what He pleases without being bound by human rules.'[93] The first generations of pious Moslems were far too preoccupied with the dread prospect of hell-fire[94] 'fearing a day when hearts and eyes shall be turned about'—to indulge the hope that the arbitrary Ruler of the universe might disclose Himself in love to His miserable and impotent slaves. But in due course, it may be through Christian influence, increasing notice was taken of those passages in the sacred Book which put God's dealings with man in a less terrible light:[95]

> And when My servants question thee
> concerning Me—I am near to answer
> the call of the caller, when he calls
> to Me; so let them respond to Me.

So the early mystics, from the end of the eighth century onwards, began to talk boldly of conversing with God, and of God speaking to them. 'These two are the qualities of the intimate: that he is disgusted with people and mankind, and finds delight in solitude and loneliness. Being in a darkened house, he abhors a light when he sees one; he closes his door, and draws his curtain, and is alone with his heart. He grows familiar with his Lord's nearness, and becomes intimate with Him, taking delight in secret converse with Him; he frees himself from any visitation which might come upon him and spoil his solitude. Yes, then one may see him dismayed even by the shining of the sun, when it enters upon him at his prayers; grievous to him is the company of other men, for they weary him; to sit with them and meet them is for him a grief and a loss. But when night covers him, and all eyes are sleeping, when every movement is stilled, and the senses of all things are quiet, then he is alone with his sorrow, and his disquietude is stirred; his sighs mount swiftly up, and long he moans, demanding the fulfilment of what his Expectation promised him, and the benefits and loving kindnesses whereby He has aforetime sustained him. Then he obtains some part of his request, and a portion of his wants is satisfied.'[96] Finally the day came when al-Ḥallāj (d. 309/922) dared to declare that his direct awareness of God was for him a clearer proof than both revelation and reason:[97]

Now stands no more between the Truth and me
Or reasoned demonstration,
Or proof, or revelation;
Now, brightly blazing forth, Truth's luminary
Hath driven out of sight
Each flickering, lesser light.

He only knoweth God, whom God hath shown
Himself; shall the eternal
Be known of the diurnal?
Not in His handiwork may God be known;
Can endless time be pent
Into a chance event?

Of Him, through Him, and unto Him, a sign
Of truth, an attestation
He grants through inspiration;
Of Him, through Him, His own, a truth divine,
A knowledge proved and sure
Hath made our hearts secure.

This I have proven, this I now declare,
This is my faith unbending,
And this my joy unending:
There is no god but God! No rivals share
His peerless majesty,
His claimed supremacy.

When men have been alone with God, and know,
This is their tongues' expression
And this their hearts' confession;
This ecstasy of joy knits friend and foe
In common brotherhood,
Working to common good.

It is true that al-Ḥallāj paid with his life for the publication of his union with the Divine Lover. But his sublime experience was being shared by an increasing band of Moslems who, weary alike of dogma and dialectic, ventured upon the perilous but joyful 'flight of the alone to the Alone.'[98] The testimony of so great a cloud of witnesses could not go unheeded. In the end that Shāfi'ī of Shāfi'īs, that Ash'arī of Ash'arīs, the Proof of Islam Muḥammad ibn Muḥammad al-Ghazālī (d. 505/1111), having tried all other ways to salvation turned away from the wranglings of the theologians and the hair-splittings of the philosophers. 'Conscious of my helplessness and having surrendered my will entirely, I took refuge with God as a man in sore trouble who has no resource left. God answered my prayer and made it easy for me to turn my back on reputation and wealth and wife and children and friends.'[99] Having studied the lives and sayings of the Sufis, he found that 'all their outward actions and inward states are irradiated by the light of the lamp of prophecy, and there is not on the face of the earth any other light from which illumination should be sought.'[100] So, when he had persevered to the end with the hard ascetic training recommended by the mystics, he too experienced the miraculous illumination vouchsafed to the saints, and urgently invited all who would follow him to climb the steep ascent to personal communion with God.[101]

So Truth is known in ecstasy,
For Truth shall evermore prevail,
And even the greatest mind must fail
To comprehend this mystery.

NOTES

[1] Not the least merit of these two pioneering works is that they contain full and excellent bibliographies to which the student is referred.

[2] E. Gilson, *Reason and Revelation in the Middle Ages*, p. 95.

[3] Plato, *Laws* 885b. The translation is that of Benjamin Jowett.

[4] *Ibid.* 887c.

[5] *Ibid.* 821a.

[6] Aristotle, *Metaphysics* 1073a.

[7] Plato, *Timaeus* 28c.

[8] Aristotle, *Nicomachean Ethics* 1178b (tr. W. D. Ross).

[9] J. Baillie, *Our Knowledge of God*, p. 119.

[10] *Ibid.* p. 120.

[11] *Ibid.* p. 123.

[12] J. W. Sweetman, *Islam and Christian Theology*, i, p. 52.

[13] Harnack, *History of Dogma*, ii, p. 228.

[14] Tertullian, *On Prescription against Heretics*, ch. 7.

[15] H. M. Gwatkin, *The Knowledge of God and its Historical Development*, i, p. 39.

[16] In *Revelation* (ed. J. Baillie and Hugh Martin), p. 117.

[17] See for instance A. Guillaume, *Islam*, p. 63.

[18] Koran iii, 138.

[19] H. M. Gwatkin, *op. cit.*, i, p. 155.

[20] Koran xii 1, xxvi 1, xxviii 1, etc.

[21] A. J. Wensinck, *The Muslim Creed*, p. 53.

[22] See especially W. M. Watt, *Free Will and Predestination in Early Islam.*

[23] Koran iii 187.

[24] J. Baillie, *Revelation*, p. xviii.

[25] W. M. Horton in *Revelation*, p. 254.

[26] *Psalms* 19: 1.

[27] Koran xxx 19-24.

[28] Koran xx 128.

[29] Koran iv 162–3.

[30] *Hebrews* 1: 1–2.

[31] Koran i 2–12.

[32] Koran xvi 126. For the use made by Averroes of this verse to support his thesis on the three types of argument, see his *Faṣl al-maqāl* (ed. L. Gauthier), p. 8.

[33] See S. van den Bergh, *Averroes' Tahafut al-Tahafut*, ii, p. 1.

[34] See I. Goldziher, *Die Richtungen der islamischen Koranauslegung.*

[35] Sufi commentaries on the Koran were written by, among others, Sahl ibn 'Abd Allāh al-Tustarī, al-Sulamī and al-Qushairī; the systematic study of these commentaries has yet to be undertaken.

[36] See especially his *Tafsīr al-Ṣamadīya.*

[37] R. Paret in *Encyclopaedia of Islam*, iv, pp. 703–4.

[38] H. A. R. Gibb, *Mohammedanism*, p. 122. The Ismā'īlīs in particular made much capital out of this claim.

[39] Averroes, *Faṣl al-maqāl*, pp. 10–11.

[40] Especially in the works by Sweetman and Gardet-Anawati to which reference has been made above.

[41] J. W. Sweetman, *op. cit.*, i, pp. 84–92.

[42] G. E. von Grunebaum, *Islam*, p. 113.

[43] A. J. Wensinck in *Encyclopaedia of Islam*, ii, p. 1052.

[44] I. Goldziher in *Encyclopaedia of Islam*, ii, p. 103.

[45] W. Bacher, *Die älteste Terminologie der jüdischen Schriftauslegung*, p. 44.

[46] See C. Brockelmann, *Geschichte der arabischen Litteratur*, Suppl. i, pp. 370, 376.

[47] J. Schacht, *The Origins of Muhammadan Jurisprudence*, pp. 99–100.

[48] See C. Brockelmann, *op. cit.*, Suppl. i, p. 235.

[49] Ibn al-Biṭrīq was working about 200/815, and Ibn Nā'ima about 220/835. Ḥunain ibn Isḥāq died in 260/873, Isḥāq ibn Ḥunain in 298/910, and Qusṭā ibn Lūqā in 300/912.

[50] In his *Risāla fī 'l-ṣaḥāba*; see J. Schacht, *op. cit.*, p. 102.

[51] See I. Goldziher in *Encyclopaedia of Islam*, i, p. 189.

[52] See D. B. Macdonald, *Development of Moslem Theology*, pp. 270–8.

[53] In *Die Mu'taziliten oder die Freidenker im Islam* (Leipzig, 1865).

[54] In *Geschichte der herrschenden Ideen des Islams* (Leipzig, 1868).

[55] A good bibliography is given by H. S. Nyberg in *Encyclopaedia of Islam*, iii, pp. 792–3.

[56] See W. M. Patton, *Aḥmad ibn Ḥanbal and the Miḥna.*

[57] Bacon, *Essays*, xvi.

[58] In his *al-Ibāna 'an uṣūl al-diyāna*; see Gardet-Anawati, *op. cit.*, p. 143.

[59] Koran v 69, cf. iii 66, xxiii 90, xxxvi 83, xxxviii 75, xlviii 10, lvii 1, 29.

[60] Koran xi 39, cf. xx 39, xxiii 27, lii 48, liv 14.

[61] Koran ii 109, cf. ii 274, vi 52, xxviii 88, lv 27.

[62] Koran x 3, cf. vii 52, xiii 2, xx 4, xxv 60, xxxii 3, lvii 4.

[63] A. S. Tritton, *Muslim Theology*, p. 48.

[64] J. W. Sweetman, *op. cit.*, ii, p. 30.

[65] A. J. Wensinck, *The Muslim Creed*, pp. 67–8, translating al-Ash'arī, *Maqālāt al-Islāmīyīn*, p. 197.

[66] P. Hitti, *Histor of the Arabs*, p. 246.

[67] John of Damascus, *Exposition of the Orthodox Faith* (tr. S. D. F. Salmond), p. 13.
[68] J. W. Sweetman, *op. cit.*, ii, p. 30; cf. A. S. Tritton, *op. cit.*, p. 24.
[69] A. J. Wensinck, *op. cit.*, p. 86.
[70] Moh. Ben Cheneb in *Encyclopaedia of Islam*, ii, p. 422.
[71] In his *al-Ibāna*, quoted by A. J. McCarthy, *The Theology of al-Ash'ari*, pp. 237–8.
[72] A. J. Wensinck, *op. cit.*, p. 73.
[73] See above.
[74] A. J. Wensinck, *op. cit.*, p. 77; see J. W. Sweetman, *op. cit.*, ii, p. 117.
[75] H. A. R. Gibb, *Mohammedanism*, pp. 111–2.
[76] See for instance R. Bell, *Introduction to the Qur'ān*, p. 37; for a sounder exposition see J. W. Sweetman, *op. cit.*, ii, p. 119.
[77] For the doctrine of *i'jāz* see Gardet-Anawati, *op. cit.*, p. 41.
[78] Koran lxxxv 22.
[79] A. J. McCarthy, *op. cit.*, pp. 20–21.
[80] A. J. Wensinck, *op. cit.*, p. 186.
[81] See al-Suyūtī, *al-La'āli' al-maṣnū'a*, i, p. 4.
[82] *Ikhlisās al-Qur'ān bi-'audihi ilā 'l-Raḥīm al-Raḥmān*, unique MS. in the library of Sir Chester Beatty.
[83] Cf. al-Suyūtī, *op. cit.*, i, p.8.
[84] See Ibn Māja, al-Sunan.
[85] This view was also shared by al-Shāfi'ī, see J. W. Sweetman, *op. cit.*, ii, 117.
[86] See A. S. Tritton, *op. cit.*, p. 105.
[87] In a *fatwā* contained in Ibn Taimīya, *Majmū'at al-rasā'il wa'l-masā'il* (ed. M. Rashīd Riḍā), ii, pp. 131-45.
[88] A. J. Wensinck, *op. cit.*, p. 187.
[89] *Ibid.*, p. 127.
[90] *Ibid.*, p. 246.
[91] *Ibid.*, p. 189.
[92] G. Galloway, *Faith and Reason in Revelation*, p. 86.
[93] A. J. Wensinck, *op. cit.*, p. 84.
[94] Koran xxiv 37.
[95] Koran ii 182.
[96] See al-Kharrāz, *The Book of Truthfulness* (tr. A. J. Arberry), p. 48.
[97] See al-Kalābādhī, *The Doctrine of the Sufis* (tr. A. J. Arberry), pp. 48–9.
[98] Plotinus, *Enneads*, v 11.
[99] See R. A. Nicholson, *The Idea of Personality in Islam*, p. 41.
[100] *Ibid.*, pp. 43–4.
[101] See al-Kalābādhī, *op. cit.*, p. 137.

II

'WISDOM is the believer's straying camel; he takes it from wherever he may find it, and does not care from what vessel it has issued.' The philosophers of Islam, like the theologians, had no difficulty in finding the appropriate sayings of the Prophet to justify their activities.[1] The identification of wisdom with philosophy seemed the simplest step in the world to take; and we need not therefore be too surprised to find al-Kindī (d. *ca.* 256/870) beginning his famous letter to the caliph al-Mu'taṣim with an enthusiastic defence of his trade—after all the traditionists, the lawyers and the theologians were accustomed to doing the same.[2] 'The sublimest and noblest of human crafts is the craft of philosophy, which may be defined as the knowledge of things in their realities to the limit of human power.'[3] So the first of the Arabian philosophers was able to embroider Mohammed's alleged encouragement of the pursuit of wisdom, and thereafter to pen the most eloquent tribute to the ancient thinkers ever written in Islam. 'It therefore behoves us to express our utmost thanks to those who have brought us even a little truth, not to mention those who have brought us much. For they have made us partakers with them in the fruits of their meditations, and eased for us the attainment of true and hidden goals, by succouring us with those preliminaries which have smoothed for us the paths to truth. . . . We ought not to be ashamed of applauding the truth, nor of appropriating the truth, from whatever source it may come, even if it be from remote races and nations alien to us. There is nothing that beseems the seeker after truth better than truth itself. Truth should never be held in light esteem, nor should we belittle him who utters it or communicates it. No one was ever cheapened by the truth; on the contrary, the truth ennobles every man.'[4]

The truth, as al-Kindī saw it, was to restate accurately what Plato, Aristotle and the other Greek sages had laboured to elucidate, and thereafter 'to complete what the ancients have not fully expressed, according to the usage of our language and the custom of our times, so far as we are able.'[5] For the Greek philosophers, whose works were in large measure available to him in translation, taught the unity of God and the pursuit of virtue, 'and the acquisition of all those things is the very substance of what the true Messengers have brought us from God.'[7] He never doubted for a moment that the harmony of the findings of Greek philosophy with the revelations of the Koran could be fully established, given the necessary good-will and patient research. It was to this end, for instance, that he undertook to expound for his pupil Aḥmad, son of al-Mu'taṣim, the true meaning of Koran LV 5:

> And the stars and the trees bow themselves.

'By my life, the utterance of Mohammed the true, and the message that he delivered from Almighty God—that is all ascertainable by intellectual processes, which are rejected by none but those deprived of the form of reason.'[8] It was essentially a linguistic question; the word 'bow' could be used to mean 'obey'—good Arabic verses might be cited to prove the fact; when applied to stars and trees it was obviously not to be understood in its technical connotation as describing a certain phase of ritual prayer. This observation leads al-Kindī into a discussion of the nature and function of the stars; as active causes in the maintenance of life on earth they obeyed the will of God. Using an ingenious syllogism, he demonstrates that the stellar system is a living and intelligent organism, and from that passes on to the familiar idea of man as the microcosm mirroring the macrocosm about him.[9]

One of the most interesting of al-Kindī's recently recovered treatises is his catalogue of the works of Aristotle. This proves a tolerably complete and detailed acquaintance with the contents of the *corpus;* is is noteworthy that some of the titles are rendered into Arabic in a manner quite different to that followed by later philosophers; in particular it is to be remarked that no mention is made of the so-called *Theology*, though al-Kindī is commonly reported to have revised Nā'ima's translation of this Neoplatonic compilation.[10] The list is interrupted for a disquisition on the sciences needing study by the philosopher; these are many and involve much labour, as contrasted with the science bestowed by God upon the prophets exclusively, which they possess 'without seeking or effort or research, without delving into mathematics and logic, and without lapse of time, but simply according to His almighty will, purifying their souls and enlightening them by His succour and guidance, His inspiration and messages.'[11] As an instance of the supernatural knowledge possessed by the prophets enabling them to solve difficult problems spontaneously, al-Kindī quotes the question put to Mohammed by the polytheists and the answer he gave them as prompted by God:[12]

He says, 'Who shall quicken the bones
when they are decayed?'
Say: 'He shall quicken them, who originated them
the first time; He knows all creation,
who has made for you out of the green tree
fire and lo, from it you kindle.'
Is not He, who created the heavens and earth,
able to create the like of them? Yes indeed;
He is the All-creator, the All-knowing.
His command, when He desires a thing, is to say to it
'Be,' and it is.

That was the blissful hour of philosophy's dawn in Islam. For al-Kindī it was no intellectual hardship to accept such Koranic doctrines as the creation of the world out of nothing and the resurrection of the body,[13] that were to prove such stumbling-blocks for later thinkers. Truth, the highest quest of man, was one and indivisible; the philosopher reached it after long and painful study, the prophet comprehended it in a single flash of inspiration. He wrote in the time when the Mu'tazila was still supreme, and it seems that he accepted that creed. Very different was the position of Rhazes half a century later. The Arab al-Kindī had declared unreserved loyalty to the message of the Arabian prophet; Rhazes (d. 313/925), a very typical Persian, felt no such prior obligation. Trained in the first place to be a physician, he claimed to have studied sufficiently widely and deeply to deserve to be accounted a philosopher. He admitted only one exception: 'As for mathematics, I freely concede that I have only looked into this subject to the extent that was absolutely indispensable, not wasting my time upon refinements; of set purpose, not out of incapacity for the study. If any man wishes to have my excuse on this head, I make bold to assert that the right course is in fact that which I have followed, not the one adopted by some so-called philosophers who fritter away their whole lives indulging in geometrical superfluities. If therefore the amount of knowledge I possess is not sufficient for me to deserve the name of philosopher, I should very much like to know who of my contemporaries is so qualified.'[14]

The account which Rhazes has left of his search after knowledge is surely one of the most remarkable and moving documents of the Middle Ages, and goes far to explain the impatience, not untouched by arrogance, of his attitude to theological mysteries. 'My love and passion for knowledge, and my labours to acquire the same, are familiar to all who have kept my company or seen me at my studies; from my youth up to this very time, I have not ceased to devote myself to this object. If ever I have come upon a book I have not read, or heard tell of a man I have not met, I have not turned aside to any engagement whatever—even though it has been to my great loss—before mastering that book or learning all that man knew. So great in fact have been my endeavours and endurance, that in a single year I have written as many as 20,000 pages in a script as minute as that used for amulets. I was engaged fifteen years upon my great compendium,[15] working night and day, until my sight began to fail and the nerves of my hand were paralysed, so that at the present time I am prevented from reading and writing; even so I do not give up these occupations so far as I am able, but always enlist the help of someone to read and write for me.'[16]

This was the man whom later writers, though wondering at his erudition, unanimously condemned for blasphemy. The strictures of Ibn Ḥazm the Ẓāhirite[17] and Nāṣir-i Khusrau the Ismā'īlī[18] are readily understandable; but it is not easy to condone the reaction of al-Bīrūnī the scientist, who went so far—must we regretfully suppose in order to please his fanatical Sunnī patron?—as to diagnose Rhazes' blindness as Divine retribution.[19] Of the great physician's metaphysical writings only a few fragments have survived the destructive zeal of his critics, but sufficient remains for us to reconstruct something of his theories. 'There were five eternal principles, not one, as in the other systems: the Creator, the soul of the world, matter, absolute time and absolute space'[20]—the 'Five Ancients' of the Harranians.[21] His notorious treatise *On Prophecy* has naturally disappeared; all that we know of its contents derives from hostile sources, but it is clear enough, and hardly surprising, that Rhazes taught the superiority of reason to revelation, an abominable heresy.[22] Some authorities state that in his lost *Fī 'l-'ilm al-ilāhī* he advanced a theory in support of metempsychosis, and Kraus refers to a passage in his *Philosophic Life* which he deems to confirm this report.[23] Rhazes is arguing in favour of the slaughter of carnivorous beasts and against the indiscriminate killing of domestic animals. 'The souls of animals cannot escape from their bodies but only those of men, which being the case, to liberate such souls from their bodies is tantamount to rescuing them and effecting their release. . . . If it were not for the fact that there is no hope for a soul to escape save from the human body, the judgment of reason would not have permitted their slaughter at all.'[24] But this quotation does not appear to be a particularly clear expression of the theory of transmigration; and in any case it would be quite in character for Rhazes to play with such an idea as being as reasonable —or unreasonable—as any other religious notion. His true attitude to the doctrine of the immortality of the soul seems to emerge more reliably in the last chapter of his charming treatise on ethics, the *Spiritual Physick;* there he betrays a wonderfully open mind on this most crucial of theological topics, ending with an amiable concession to placate those who believe in survival. 'Again I repeat that I have demonstrated that there is no ground for fearing death, if a man holds that there is no future state after death. And now I say that in accordance with the other view—the view that makes out a future state attendant upon death—there is also no need for a man to fear death, if he be righteous and virtuous, and carries out all the duties imposed upon him by the religious law which is true; for this law promises him victory and repose and the attainment of everlasting bliss. And if any man should doubt the truth of that law, or is ignorant of it, or is not certain that is is real, it only behoves him to search and consider to the limit of his strength and power; for if he applies all his capacity and strength, without failing or flagging, he can scarcely fail to arrive at the right goal. And if he should fail—which is scarcely likely to happen—yet Almighty God is more apt to forgive and pardon him, seeing that He requires of no man what lies not within his capacity; rather does He charge and impose upon His servants far, far less than that.'[25] On this matter, as perhaps on many others, Rhazes would doubtless have approved the lines written by a tenth century Persian poet:[26]

> To this point doth my knowledge go—
> I only know I nothing know.

In Rhazes' contemporary al-Fārābī the Turk (d. 339/950) we are confronted by a man whose primary interest was in political science, though to be sure his writings attest a wide acquaintance with all branches of Greek philosophy. His attempt to reconcile revelation with reason was chiefly directed towards interpreting in Moslem terms Plato's *Republic* and *Laws* and Aristotle's *Ethics* and *Politics*. Having established to his own satisfaction a harmony between the teachings of Plato and Aristotle[27]—a task rendered considerably easier by his acceptance of the *Theology*—he applied himself unremittingly to his chosen task. 'Philosophy was not to replace traditional religion altogether, but was to assign it its proper position as had been done in the Greek world by Plato. He tried, indeed, to re-interpret the whole of Islam from his own philosophical standpoint, using Greek philosophy as a torch which gave new light to every aspect of Islamic life: dialectical theology, creed and Qur'ān, law, jurisprudence, grammar, aesthetic appreciation of artistic prose and poetry, and above all the organisation of the perfect society and the essential qualities of its ruler. If the times were propitious, one universal world-state might come into existence; if not, several religions might exist side by side, and, if this also were impracticable, Islam at least might be reshaped according to the demands of the royal power of philosophy, which was the highest perfection of which man was capable.' Walzer's analysis of al-Fārābī's rather involved system puts the matter with admirable clarity.[28] He accepted Aristotle's definition of happiness as the supreme aim of human life; the Arabic term used to translate εὐδαιμονία, *sa'āda*, inevitably awakened Koranic echoes:[29]

> Surely in that is a sign for him who fears
> the chastisement in the world to come;
> that is a day mankind are to be gathered to,
> a day to witness,
> and We shall not postpone it, save to

a term reckoned;
the day it comes, no soul shall speak save
by His leave; some of them shall be wretched
and some happy.
As for the wretched, they shall be in the
Fire, wherein there shall be for them
moaning and sighing,
therein dwelling forever, so long as
the heavens and earth abide, save as thy
Lord will; surely thy Lord accomplishes
what He desires.
And as for the happy, they shall be in
Paradise, therein dwelling forever,
so long as the heavens and earth abide,
save as thy Lord will—for a
gift unbroken.

The word rendered by 'happy' is *sa'īd.*

How is happiness to be achieved? 'The function of the Active Intellect is to care for the rational animal and to seek to enable him to reach the furthest ranks of perfection attainable by man. That is the highest happiness; and it consists in man's persevering to the rank of the Active Intellect. This can only happen by his becoming separated from the body and not needing for his subsistence anything else, be it physical, material or accidental, and remaining in that state of perfection for ever. . . . The Active Intellect moreover is what ought to be called the Faithful Spirit, and the Spirit of Holiness.'[30] The equating of the Active Intellect with the Holy Ghost (or Gabriel) enabled al-Fārābī to construct his philosophical theory of revelation, which is manifestly derived from al-Kindī's prior statement.[31] 'The First Ruler has no need of any man at all to rule him; all science and all knowledge have accrued to him in actuality without his requiring in any way at all any man to direct him. . . . That only happens with people of great and superior temperament, when the soul of such a man has achieved union with the Active Intellect. . . . This man is truly a king, as the ancients held; it must also be said of him that he is inspired (*yūḥā ilaihi*). For a man is only inspired when he reaches this rank, namely when there remains no intermediary between him and the Active Intellect. . . . Moreover since the Active Intellect emanates (*fā'iḍ*) from the essence of the First Cause, it can therefore be said that the First Cause is the inspirer of such a man, through the mediation of the Active Intellect.'[32] In such an exalted state he receives from the Active Intellect, while actually awake, details of all matters both present and future, and he is consequently able to prophesy of Divine things (*nubūwa bi'l-ashyā' al-ilāhīya*).[33]

The Koranic version of creation is less easy to reconcile with al-Fārābī's scheme, though allegory to be sure is a wonderfully supple instrument; he adopts the Neoplatonic pattern of emanation, a descending series of secondary beings deriving their existence from the First Cause, in all eleven immaterial intelligences corresponding to the heavenly spheres and leading down finally to the sublunary world.[34] His conception of life after death appears to leave no room for the resurrection of the body. The treatment of eschatology in his most famous book, *The Views of the People of the Virtuous State*, is not lacking in confusion however, and seems to be an attempt to co-ordinate several distinct and mutually contradictory theories. The Islamic doctrine of the joy of the blessed in Paradise and the misery of the damned in Hell receives an esoteric interpretation; on the other hand the souls of the wicked are alternatively resolved into the elements, and transformed into lower animals.[35]

Since the most critical point of difference between philosophy and orthodox belief in Islam centres on the fate of the human being after death, it is instructive to compare what was written on this topic by the traditional mystic al-Muḥāsibī (d. 243/837) with what Avicenna (d.428/1037) had to say some two centuries later. The former composed in his *Kitāb al-Tawahhum* an exceedingly graphic account of the events preceding and following the separation of the soul from the body. His description of these tremendous happenings follows closely the literal teaching of the Koran, as further elaborated in the Traditions of Mohammed and the sayings of early Moslem saints. The *Dies Irae* naturally offers wide scope for the play of an imagination stimulated by such terrifying words as[36]

When the sun shall be darkened,
when the stars shall be thrown down,
when the mountains shall be set moving,
when the pregnant camels shall be neglected,
when the savage beasts shall be mustered,
when the seas shall be set boiling,
when the souls shall be coupled,
when the buried infant shall be asked for what sin she was slain,
when the scrolls shall be unrolled,
when heaven shall be stripped off,
when Hell shall be set blazing,
when Paradise shall be brought nigh,
then shall a soul know what it has produced.

After the agony of death, as al-Muḥāsibī envisages the matter, the soul is subjected to the rigorous inquisition of Munkar and Nakīr, the two 'angels of the grave,' and is given a preview of Paradise or Hell according to the manner in which it acquits itself at this sharp questioning. Then follows the dissolution of the body, while the soul awaits in eagerness or trepidation for 'the number of the dead to be completed, and earth and heaven to be emptied of their inhabitants. Then no sound shall be heard, nor any shape seen, and the Omnipotent and Most High shall abide as He has ever been, One and Solitary in His majesty and glory.'[37] Suddenly a single shout goes up, summoning all creatures to the Judgment, and the mighty throng of men and beasts hastens in all humility to the appointed place.

As they stand there rank on rank, 'the stars of heaven shall be scattered above them, and the sun and moon shall be obliterated, and the earth shall be darkened because of the extinguishing of its lantern and the putting out of its light.'[38] The lower heaven will be split asunder with a tremendous roar, and converted as it were into molten silver flecked with yellow;[39] the troops of angels will swoop down out of the clouds. The dimensions of the occasion are illustrated by a *ḥadīth* to the effect that God has one angel so huge that the distance between the rims of his two eyes is a hundred years' journey.[40] Yet even these mighty angels are bowed in awe and subjection as they await the advent of their Lord.

Dreadful will be the pressing and jostling of the myriads of bodies, immense the anguish of their thirst in that intolerable heat. The sweat will pour from the assembled multitudes until it covers the entire surface of the earth; some will be inundated by it up to their ankles, some to their loins, some to the lobes of their ears, while some will suffer an almost total submersion. All these details are supported by the relevant Traditions. There was a difference of opinion between the Prophet's Companions as to how long this painful waiting is to last; Qutāda (or Ka'b) estimated it at 300 years, whereas al-Ḥasan put the figure at 50,000 years.[41] At last the interval will come to an end, following the intercession of Mohammed, and each individual will be summoned by name to the bar of Divine justice. So the awful panorama of the Day of Decision unrolls itself, the author's wealth of rhetorical imagery being always justified by reliable reports and apposite Koranic quotations. The Judgment is enacted, and every creature is separately assigned to Hell or Paradise; the fires of Divine wrath blaze with unimaginable fierceness. Then the soul acquitted of its sins hastens tremblingly over the bridge hung between Paradise and Hell, and descries with overwhelming joy the celestial pleasures promised by God to the faithful righteous. It passes through the portals of the heavenly garden—their width is the distance of a forty years' journey—and is immediately welcomed by the denizens of Paradise created by God to minister to the comforts of His beatified servants, no fewer than 70,000 being assigned to the service of each.[42] 'Imagine the scene that will confront you when you open the doors of your palace, and raise the curtains—the lovely chambers, the decorative trees, the beautiful meadows, the glittering area, the gleaming courts. Then, while you are still gazing at that, your servants will hasten with the glad news, proclaiming to your wives, "Behold, So-and-so has entered the door of his palace." When they hear the proclamation of those bearing the good tidings of your arrival, they will leap from their couches spread within the bridal apartments; and you will see them there in the hollow of the tents and tabernacles, leaping up and hastening with joy and ardour to behold you. Imagine those soft and supple bodies as they leap up and sway gracefully towards you. . . . Then each one of them will cry out, "My beloved, what has delayed so long your coming to us?" '[43] So the tender scene continues, pictured in terms outrivalling the description of some mighty caliph's wedding. All memory of the anguish of the Judgment Day is blotted out in the overmastering ecstasy of the ensuing revel, rendered all the more delightful by the first tasting of the wines of Paradise.

The long carouse is interrupted by the arrival of angelic messengers bearing precious gifts from God: 'Friend of God, thy Lord greets thee and sends thee these gifts and presents.'[44] The angels depart, and the bridal feast is resumed with renewed enthusiasm; until finally God announces that He desires to consummate His promise to His saints and to accord them the incomparable joy of entering His Presence. A caravan of dromedaries, fashioned of rubies and with bridles of gold, awaits to convey the happy souls of the saved upon their last journey. One remarkable feature of these miraculous winged beasts is that they neither stale nor dung.[45] The blessed servants of the Most High, with jewelled crowns about their brows, mount into the saddles of pearls and rubies, and the splendid procession sets forth. A superb banquet is spread against their coming, and they are privileged to be partakers of the Divine hospitality.[46] After they have eaten and drunk to their satisfaction, the attendant angels clothe them in new apparel and sprinkle them with heavenly scents. 'Then the curtains are lifted, and their Lord appears to them in all His perfection. When they gaze upon Him, and upon That which they never have and never shall have so much as imagined—for He is the Eternal One, whom naught of His creation is like unto—when they gaze upon Him, then will their Beloved bid them be welcome, saying, "Welcome to My servants!" And having heard God's words, in all their majesty and beauty, their hearts will be overcome with joy and happiness such as they never knew before, whether in the lower world or in Paradise; for they will be listening to the speech of Him who is like unto no other thing. Imagine them therefore, as with downcast eyes they hearken attentively to His words, while the light of joy irradiates their countenances because of the words spoken by their Beloved are their Delight. . . . Then He will greet them again (and they will answer Him saying, "Thou art the All-peaceable;[47] from Thee peace proceeds, and Thou art worthy of awe and reverence"): "Welcome to My servants and visitors, to My chosen ones out of all My creation, who have kept My covenant and preserved My trust, fearing Me in the Unseen and being ever in lively dread of Me. For I have seen how they laboured when they were in the body, preferring that I should be well-pleased with them. I saw what the people of your time did with you, and how the cruelty of men did not prevent you from paying Me My due. Desire of Me what you will!". . . Thereupon they will say, "By Thy might and majesty, by Thy omnipotence and sublimity, we never measured Thee with Thy true measure, neither have we paid Thee all Thy due. Give us leave, that we may prostrate ourselves before Thee." But their Lord will say to them, "I have now laid aside from your backs the burden of service; I have given ease to your bodies. Long time indeed did you weary your bodies, and humble to Me your faces. Now you have won through to My bounty and My mercy; therefore desire whatsoever you will!" '[48] Then God will give His saints leave to depart, and they will return every one to his palace, there to enjoy for evermore the ineffable delights of Paradise.

Such was the mystic al-Muḥāsibī's vision of the last things. It was a vision justified by the words of Moslem revelation; and he was certainly in the great majority in taking the Koranic message for a literal prophecy.[49] Though the Ḥanbalīs joined issue with him on a number of points including his doctrine of the direct vision of God in Paradise,[50] the Ash'arīs and the Shāfi'īs welcomed him as one whose views were free of contamination with the outrageous opinions of the philosophers.[51] Indeed his full-blooded description of the heavenly reward makes the Neoplatonist conception of some austere union with the Active Intellect seem a little anaemic by comparison. To challenge the verbal accuracy of such passages in the Koran as Sura LV 46–61:

> But such as fears the Station of his Lord,
> for them shall be two gardens—
> O which of your Lord's bounties will you and you deny?
> abounding in branches—
> O which of your Lord's bounties will you and you deny?
> therein two fountains of running water—
> O which of your Lord's bounties will you and you deny?
> therein of every fruit two kinds—
> O which of your Lord's bounties will you and you deny?
> reclining upon couches lined with brocade,
> the fruits of the gardens nigh to gather—
> O which of your Lord's bounties will you and you deny?
> therein maidens restraining their glances,
> untouched before them by any man or jinn—
> O which of your Lord's bounties will you and you deny?

lovely as rubies, beautiful as coral—
O which of your Lord's bounties will you and you deny?
Shall the recompense of goodness be other than goodness?
O which of your Lord's bounties will you and you deny?

to challenge the authenticity of such a promise, in a time when orthodoxy was triumphant, surely called for intellectual courage of an exceptional order. That is the background against which Avicenna's cool and detached observations are to be assessed.

'The after-life is a notion received from religious teaching; there is no way of establishing its truth save by way of religious dogma and acceptance of the prophets' reports as true; these refer to what will befall the body at the resurrection, and those corporeal delights or torments which are too well known to require restating here. The true religion brought into this world by our Prophet Muḥammad has described in detail the state of happiness or misery awaiting us hereafter so far as the body is concerned. Some further support for the idea of a hereafter is attainable through reason and logical demonstration—and this is confirmed by prophetic teaching—namely, that happiness or misery posited by spiritual appraisement; though it is true that our conjecture falls short of realising a full picture of them now, for reasons which we shall explain. Metaphysicians have a greater desire to achieve this spiritual happiness than the happiness which is purely physical; indeed they scarcely heed the latter, and were they granted it would not consider it of great moment in comparison with the former kind, which is proximity to the First Truth, in a manner to be described presently. Let us therefore consider this state of happiness, and of contrasting misery: the physical sort is fully dealt with in the teachings of religion.'[52]

So far Avicenna gives the impression of a man with an open mind. But he proceeds to argue the superiority of the philosopher's conception of Heaven and Hell. 'It behoves not the intelligent man to suppose that every pleasure is connected with the belly and the sexual instinct, as is the case with asses; that the First Principles, which dwell in close proximity to the Lord of All, are wholly without pleasure and exultation; or that Almighty God in His Sublime Splendour and Infinite Power does not enjoy a State of Noble Pre-eminence and Well-being which we reverently refrain from calling pleasure. Asses and wild beasts have it is true their own sort of well-being and pleasure; but what relation is there between these mean delights, and the sensation enjoyed by the Lofty Principles? Their beatitude we may only imagine and contemplate; we cannot know it in our conscient minds, but solely by analogy; our state being that of the deaf man who never in all his life heard or could imagine the joy of music, yet he was sure that it was truly excellent.'[63] The philosopher's celestial pleasure derives from the realisation of spiritual perfection. 'Now the peculiar perfection towards which the rational soul strives is that it should become as it were an intellectual microcosm, impressed with the form of the All, the order intelligible in the All, and the good pervading the All: first the Principle of the All, then proceeding to the Noble Substances and Absolute Spirituality, then Spirituality connected in some fashion with corporeal things, then the Celestial Bodies with their various dispositions and powers, and so continuing until it realises completely within itself the shape of all Being, and thus converts itself into an intelligible cosmos of its own in correspondence with the whole existing Cosmos, contemplating perfect Comeliness, absolute Good and true Beauty, and united therewith. So it will have become graven after its idea and pattern, and strung upon its thread as a pearl is strung upon a necklace, being refashioned into the self-same substance thereof. When this state is compared with those other perfections so ardently beloved of the other faculties, it will be found to be of an order so exalted as to make it seem monstrous to describe it as more complete and more excellent than they; indeed, there is no relation between it and them whatsoever, whether it be of excellence, completeness, abundance, or any other of the respects wherein delight in sensual attainment is consummated.'[54]

Avicenna then proposes his own version of the events that ensue after death. 'When the time comes for us to be separated from the body, and our soul has become aware while still in the body of that perfection which is the object of its love, yet has not attained it, though naturally still yearning after it, for it has in fact realised that it exists though its preoccupation with the body has caused it to forget its own essence and its true beloved (and so sickness will cause us to forget the need of replacing the parts that are dissolved within us, or even the pleasure of sweet things and the appetite for them; and unnatural desire will make a sick man incline after revolting things)—then at that time our soul is truly affected by pain at the loss of our cherished object, equal to the supervening pleasure whose existence we have proved and whose lofty rank we have indicated. This then is a misery and a torment far exceeding the bodily pain and physical anguish of burning and freezing. At that moment we are like to a man who has been drugged, or so affected by fire or cold that the material clothing his senses prevents him from feeling anything, so that he senses no discomfort for the while; but then the intervening obstacle is removed, and he is conscious of great suffering. If, however, the intellectual faculty has achieved such a degree of perfection within the soul that the latter is able, on leaving the body, to realise that full perfection which lies within its power to attain, the soul will then resemble a man drugged who is given to taste some most delicious food, or confronting him a most ravishing situation, without his being conscious of the fact; when the drug passes off, he discovers great pleasure all at once. But the pleasure enjoyed by the soul at that moment is not at all of the order of sensual or animal delight; rather does it resemble that delectable state which belongs to pure vital substances, mightier and nobler than all other pleasure.'[55]

Such is the destiny awaiting the soul which has become conscious while in the body of the nature of intellectual perfection. 'As for those foolish souls which have never acquired the yearning for perfection, yet leave the body without having acquired any vicious bodily disposition, these pass to the wide Mercy of God and attain a kind of ease. If, however, they have acquired some vicious bodily disposition and have no other condition but that, nothing within them to oppose or strive with it, then they continue inevitably to be bemused by their yearning after what is for them an absolute necessity, and are exquisitely tortured by the loss of the body and all the body's requirements without being able to attain the object of their desire. For the instrument of their desire has been destroyed, while the habit of attachment to the body still survives.'[56]

The Persian philosopher concludes with a further word on the orthodox Moslem picture of life after death. 'It may also be true, as some theologians state, that when souls, supposing they are pure, leave the body, having firmly fixed within them some such beliefs regarding the future life as are appropriate to them, being the sort of picture which can properly be presented to the ordinary man—when such men as these leave the body, lacking both the force to draw them upwards to complete perfection (so that they achieve that supreme happiness) and likewise the yearning after such perfection (so that they experience that supreme misery), but all their spiritual dispositions are turned towards the lower world and drawn to the corporeal; since there is nothing to prevent celestial matter from being operable to the action of any soul upon it, these souls may well imagine all those after-life circumstances in which they believed as actually taking place before them, the instrument reinforcing their imagination being some kind of celestial body. In this way these pure souls will really be spectators of the events of the grave and the resurrection about which they were told in this world, and all the good things of the after-life; while the wicked souls will similarly behold, and suffer, the punishment which was portrayed to them here below. Certainly the imaginative picture is no weaker than the sensual image; rather is it the stronger and clearer of the two. This may be observed in dreams: the vision seen in sleep is often of greater moment in its kind than the impression of the senses. The image contemplated in the after-life is however more stable than that seen in dreams, because there are fewer obstacles in the way of its realisation; the soul being isolated from the body, the receiving instrument is therefore absolutely clear. As you know, the image seen in dreams and that sensed in waking are alike simply impressed upon the soul; they differ only in this, that the former kind originates from within and descends into the soul, while the latter sort originates from without and mounts up into the soul. It is when the image has already been impressed upon the soul that the act of contemplation is consummated. It is this impression, then, that in reality pleases or pains the soul, not any external object; whatever is impressed upon the soul does its work, even if there be no external cause. The essential cause is the impression itself; the external object is the accidental cause, or the cause of the cause. These then are the baser sorts of celestial happiness and misery, which are opposite to base souls. As for the souls of the blessed, they are far removed from such circumstances; being perfect, they are united to the Essence, and are wholly plunged in true pleasure; they are forever free of gazing after what lies behind them, and the kingdom that once was theirs. If there had remained within them any trace of those things, whether by reason of dogmatic belief or through acceptance of a physical theory, they would be so injured thereby as to fall short of scaling the topmost peak of heaven, until that thing be finally obliterated from their souls.'[57]

The foregoing extracts, in which we seem to hear the voices of Plato and Plotinus speaking again, but in accents that much more charming for being now the expression of a Persian mind, are taken from Avicenna's popular philosophical manual, *The Book of Salvation*. He also wrote a monograph, for the benefit of a particular friend, in which he reviewed all the eschatological theories known to him and set forth in clear and vigorous language his own final views. This essay, *al-Risālat al-aḍḥawīya fī amr al-ma'ād*, is of capital importance for the notice taken of it by al-Ghazālī in his *Incoherence of the Philosophers*; it has recently been published for the first time by an Egyptian scholar.[58] Avicenna argues at length that it would have been useless for any prophet to preach a purely spiritual resurrection if the masses of mankind were to be moved to pursue virtue. Physical pleasure and physical pain is what they understand; 'true happiness and spiritual pleasure are not comprehended by them at all and have no place whatever in their understandings, even though some may make a verbal pretence of it.'[59] It proves the superiority of Mohammed to all other prophets, that he painted for men the most realistic and emotive picture of heaven and hell. The Christian notion of a physical resurrection bereft of the usual delights of the flesh is particularly ineffective; such a life is the life of angels, and the private opinion of the ordinary man about angels—even if he does not dare to say so—is that their existence is miserable in the extreme. 'They have no pleasure and no repose at all; they neither eat, drink, nor marry; they are at their alleluias and devotions every hour of the night and day, never flagging for a moment, and at the end of it all they are not even rewarded.'[60] Avicenna refutes the doctrines of the resurrection of the body alone—what is to happen, for instance, in the case of a man who has been eaten by a cannibal?[61]—and of the resurrection of body and soul together; he is equally summary in his rejection of metempsychosis. In what does the personality of a man consist? Certainly not in his body; therefore it must be in his soul—and it is through the soul that the individual personality survives death. The rational soul does not depend for its existence upon matter; if this were the case, then the intelligence would diminish with the decline of the physique, whereas 'in many old men, or rather in most of them, the intellectual faculty only shows itself clearly when the body weakens, after forty-years—which is the climax of the physical powers---and especially after sixty, when the body has actually begun to grow feeble.'[62]

Thus Avicenna establishes to his own evident satisfaction that the human soul is immortal. By logical analysis he demonstrates that after death the soul will experience either everlasting happiness or everlasting misery; the customary terms employed, *sa'āda* and *shaqāwa*, recall both Aristotle and the Koran.[63] It only remains to determine the nature of that happiness and misery. This involves a discussion of pleasure and pain, on the traditional lines. 'Pleasure is the attainment of the congenial';[64] and there are various sorts of congeniality. Every sense has its own kind of pleasure, and 'true sensual pleasure is the sensation of recovery of the natural state.'[65] Now it has been proved that the rational soul is of nobler stuff than all its rival claimants for the attention of man; therefore the pleasure proper to the rational soul is the noblest and most perfect of all pleasures. Its congenial objects of perception are 'the permanent ideas, the spiritual forms, and the First Principle of all Being in His majesty and magnificence.'[66] The human soul is without doubt of angelic substance; 'and glory be to God! Are the good and the pleasure peculiar to angelic substances to be compared with the good and the pleasure peculiar to the substances of brute beasts?'[67] That high pleasure is not sensed by us while we are in the body, because the physical forces prevail over the rational soul; but as the vital powers diminish, the perception of that celestial delight begins to increase; yet it is only in the other world that it can be fully reached. 'Happiness in the world to come, when the soul has become free and stripped of the body and of physical impressions, is perfect pleasure, being the intellectual contemplation of the Essence of Him to whom belongs the kingdom most mighty, the spiritual beings who worship Him, the world most sublime, and the attainment of one's perfection thereto. Misery in the world to come is the opposite of that.'[68]

The soul that has been dominated while in the body by the lower passions is accompanied by sensual impressions into the after-life; these prevent it from achieving true perfection and happiness, and such a man 'is as if he were still in the body; it is to this fact that certain philosophers have referred allegorically when speaking of metempsychosis.'[69] Among the things that release the soul from physical defilements is 'the worship of God, and the employment of those means prescribed by the Law of the Prophet; they are a fortress and a protection for the soul against this evil.'[70] Finally, 'the most eminent theologians take the view that the purified and perfect soul has no perception of sensible things. Certain theologians however say that when the soul leaves the body, taking with it the imaginative faculty, then it is impossible for it to be stripped and freed of the body altogether, and to be unaccompanied by any physical appurtenances. So at death the soul is aware of death; after death it pictures itself as being that man who has just died, in his very form, precisely as it used to picture things in dreams. It pictures itself as buried; it pictures the pains coming upon it, after the fashion of conventional sensual punishments, and all those things it believed while alive would come to pass. . . . This is the "chastisement and reward of the grave."[71] As for the "Second Growth,"[72] that they say is his emergence from the garb of that environment, namely the grave. It will be no wonder, therefore, if there appear to a man in the next world, before the "Second Growth" and after it, those phenomena mentioned in the books of the prophets, such as heavenly gardens, dark-eyed maidens and the like—all that of course according to the favourable picture.'[73]

This is the boldest and most persuasive argument in favour of a spiritual and against a physical survival to be found in Arabic literature. Avicenna laboured sincerely and ingeniously to effect a harmony between reason and revelation on these Neoplatonic lines. If his interpretation of the doctrine of personal immortality had prevailed, the subsequent history of Moslem thought would assuredly have been very different. It is possible that Greek philosophy would have continued upon its vitalising course, and Islam might never have known a Dark Age. On the other hand it may well be that, given the physics and astronomy inherited from the ancient world, human reason had reached its speculative limit with Avicenna and could not take another leap forward until Copernicus and Newton transformed men's picture of the universe. However that may be, the orothodox theologians of the eleventh century could not dare to let Avicenna have the last word; allegorisation was all very well if kept within strict bounds, but there were certain things they felt it would be far too dangerous to have explained away. To be sure Avicenna himself, like al-Fārābī before him, had also been conscious of the peril involved in allowing too wide publicity to such unconventional notions; the Moslem philosophers cheerfully advocated the expediency of permitting one truth for the masses, and another truth for the elect.[74] The theologians saw clearly enough where that kind of double-talk might also lead; the only safe course, as they thought, and perhaps rightly, in a world menaced by political disruption and beset by growing doubt, was to uphold the pure tradition of one truth sufficient for all men, the truth of the Koran. That was God's undoubted speech, as communicated to His chosen Messenger; and the plain words of the Almighty were a surer guide for perplexed humanity than all the airy theorisings of Plato and Aristotle and their latter-day exponents.[75]

> Believers, God has sent down to you, for a remembrance, a Messenger reciting to you the signs of God, clear signs, that He may bring forth those who believe and do righteous deeds from the shadows into the light. Whosoever believes in God, and does

righteousness, He will admit him to gardens underneath which rivers flow; therein they shall dwell for ever and ever. God has made for him a goodly provision.

NOTES

[1] Abū Rīda, *Rasā'il al-Kindī al-falsafīya*, p. 50.

[2] A perusal of the exordia of many manuals establishes the popularity of this conventional claim.

[3] Abū Rīda, *op. cit.*, p. 97.

[4] *Ibid.*, pp. 102–3.

[5] *Ibid.*, p. 103.

[6] See especially al-Kindī's tract *Fī kamīya kutub Arisṭūṭālis*, ed. Abū Rīda in *op. cit.*, pp. 363–84.

[7] *Ibid.*, p. 104.

[8] *Ibid.*, p. 244.

[9] This notion was afterwards taken up by the authors of the *Rasā'il Ikhwān al-Ṣafā'*, and passed into Sufi theosophy through Ibn 'Arabī.

[10] See J. W. Sweetman, *Islam and Christian Theology*, i, p. 91.

[11] Abū Rīda, *op. cit.*, pp. 372–3.

[12] Koran xxxvi 78–82.

[13] See R. Walzer in *History of Philosophy: Eastern and Western*, ii, pp. 131–2.

[14] *The Spiritual Physick of Rhazes* (tr. A. J. Arberry), p. 15.

[15] The reference is to al-Rāzī's *al-Ḥāwī*, known in the Middle Ages as the *Continens*.

[16] *The Spiritual Physick of Rhazes*, p. 16.

[17] For the references to his *al-Fiṣal*, see P. Kraus and S. Pines, *Encyclopaedia of Islam*, iii, p. 1136.

[18] *Ibid.*

[19] See al-Bīrūnī, Risāla (ed. P. Kraus), p. 5.

[20] R. Walzer in *op. cit.*, ii, p. 135.

[21] See P. Kraus, *Razis Opera Philosophica*, pp. 195–216.

[22] Fragments in P. Kraus, *op. cit.*

[23] *Ibid.*, pp. 175–6.

[24] See *The Asiatic Review*, July 1949, pp. 707–8.

[25] *The Spiritual Physick of Rhazes*, pp. 106–7.

[26] Abū Shakūr of Balkh (fl. A.D. 950), see *Legacy of Persia*, p. 227.

[27] In his *al-Jam' baina ra'yai al-Ḥakīmain*.

[28] In *op. cit.*, ii, p. 136.

[29] Koran xi 105–110.

[30] See al-Fārābī, *al-Siyāsāt al-madanīya*, p. 3. The term 'Faithful Spirit' (= Gabriel) occurs in Koran xxvi 193; 'Spirit of Holiness' (= Holy Ghost) occurs in Koran ii 81, 254, v 109, xvi 104. In his *Ārā' ahl al-*

madinat al-fāḍila (Cairo, 1907), p. 53, al-Fārābī has human perfection stop short of the rank of the Active Intellect.

31 See above, p. 36.

32 See *al-Siyāsāt al-madaniya*, pp. 49–50.

33 *Ārā' ahl al-madinat al-fāḍila*, p. 59.

34 *Ibid.*, pp. 21–26.

35 *Ibid.*, pp. 71–75.

36 Koran lxxxi 1–14.

37 See al-Muḥāsibī, *Kitāb al-Tawahhum*, p. 4.

38 *Ibid.*, p. 6.

39 Cf. Koran lv 37.

40 *Kitāb al-Tawahhum*, p. 7.

41 *Ibid.*, pp. 9–10.

42 *Ibid.*, p. 40.

43 *Ibid.*, pp. 41–2.

44 *Ibid.*, p. 49.

45 *Ibid.*, p. 53.

46 Cf. Koran iii 197, xviii 107, xxxii 19, xxxvii 60, xli 32.

47 Koran lix 23.

48 *Kitāb al-Tawahhum*, pp. 59–60.

49 We shall see that al-Ghazālī made this a crucial point in his attack on the philosophers, see below, p. 63.

50 See L. Massignon in *Encyclopaedia of Islam*, iii, p. 699.

51 See al-Subkī, *Ṭabaqāt al-Shāfi'iya*, ii, p. 42.

52 A. J. Arberry, *Avicenna on Theology*, p. 64.

53 *Ibid.*, pp. 65–6.

54 *Ibid.*, p. 67.

55 *Ibid.*, pp. 69–70.

56 *Ibid.*, p. 74.

57 *Ibid.*, pp. 75–6.

58 Sulaimān Dunyā, Cairo, 1368/1949.

59 *Op. cit.*, p. 62, cf. p. 97.

60 *Ibid.*, pp. 61–2.

61 *Ibid.*, p. 56.

62 *Ibid.*, p. 106.

63 See above, pp. 40–1.

64 *Op. cit.*, p. 112.

65 *Ibid.*, p. 113.

66 *Ibid.*, p. 116.

67 *Ibid.*, p. 117.

68 *Ibid.*, pp. 117–8.

[69] *Ibid.*, p. 119.

[70] *Ibid.*, p. 120.

[71] The examination of the departed soul by the angels Munkar and Nakīr.

[72] Cf. Koran xxix 19, liii 48, lvi 62.

[73] *Op. cit.*, pp. 124–5.

[74] This viewpoint is particularly advanced by Averroes in his *Faṣl al-maqāl*.

[75] Koran lxv 11.

III

It fell to al-Ghazālī, a fellow-Persian hailing from the same northern province as Avicenna, to deal the fatal blow to philosophy in Islam; his qualifications to be executioner-in-chief were a mind of extraordinary suppleness, a truly devastating gift for polemic, a high degree of sincerity which did not prevent him from being quite ruthless if need be, and an acute sensitivity to the changing temper of the times. His main attack, the climax to a series of preliminary preparations,[1] was delivered in the famous *Incoherence of the Philosophers*[2] in which he took his opponents to task on twenty separate points, beginning with creation and ending with the last things. He approached his congenial engagement with a superb self-confidence unaffected by any lingering reverence for those Greek giants whose legend had so strangely bemused the minds of his philosophising predecessors. 'The source of their infidelity was their hearing terrible names such as Socrates and Hippocrates, Plato and Aristotle'—the Arabic forms lend themselves to lively ridicule, Suqrāṭ wa-Buqrāṭ wa-Aflāṭūn wa-Arisṭūṭālīs; and listen to the catalogue of their boasted sciences: *al-handasiya wa-l-manṭiqiya wa-ṭ-ṭabī'iya wa-l-ilāhīya,* 'mathematical and logical, physical and metaphysical.' Their duped followers, whose unbelief rested on no more secure foundations than the blind acceptance of traditional dogma such as that which had led the Jews and Christians astray, delight to 'relate of them how, with all the gravity of their intellects and the exuberance of their erudition, they denied the sacred laws and creeds and rejected the details of the religions and faiths, believing them to be fabricated ordinances and bedizened trickeries.'[3] So much for the earnest attempts of al-Fārābī and Avicenna to enlist Greek learning to the providing of an intellectual basis for Islam.

One by one al-Ghazālī lays bare the points on which the philosophers can be convicted of incoherence; for it is a clear proof of the unreliability of their conclusions that, whereas in mathematics they construct their theorems on sound demonstrations entirely free of conjecture and so reach results on which there is common agreement, when it comes to metaphysics they are all at cross purposes. Why, it was their favourite hero Aristotle himself who said, with reference to his own teacher Plato, 'Plato is a friend, and truth is a friend, but truth is a greater friend than he.'[4] The long argument is at last brought to a close with a brief concluding section. 'If someone should say, "Now that you have set forth these men's doctrines in detail, do you reach the categorical view that they are to be declared infidels, and that anyone adopting their beliefs ought to be put to death?" we would reply, "They are absolutely to be condemned as infidels on three counts. The first of these is the question of the eternity of the world, and their statement that all substances are eternal; the second is their assertion that God does not encompass in His knowledge particular events occurring to individuals;[5] the third is their denial of the resurrection of the body." '[6] Presumably then al-Ghazālī would concur in the execution of any man who made a public declaration that the body did not share with the soul in immortality.

This is his twentieth topic in the *Incoherence*, and he sets it up on the following lines. 'To refute their denial of the resurrection of the body and the return of the soul to its physical frame, the existence of a physical hell, the existence of paradise and the houris, and the rest of what mankind has been promised, together with their assertion that all that is mere parables coined for the common people and intended to connote a spiritual reward and retribution, these being higher in rank than the corporeal. This,' al-Ghazālī states firmly, 'is contrary to the beliefs of all Moslems.'[7] He opens the case with a summary of Avicenna's arguments—he quotes his actual words liberally, though he does not mention him by name—and he begins his reply with a concession; he is prepared to grant much of what the philosophers say, and in particular their assertion that 'in the other world there are varieties of pleasure that are greater than sense-impressions.'[8] He takes his stand however upon revelation, and opposes the philosophers' exclusive reliance on reason. Why should not the two sorts of happiness and misery anyhow be combined, the spiritual and the bodily?[9] After all, God has said:[10]

> No soul knows what comfort is laid up
> for them secretly.

There is also the Divine promise: 'I have prepared for My righteous servants what eye hath not seen, nor ear heard, neither hath it entered into the heart of man.'[11] The argument that the descriptions of the other world occurring in the Koran are to be taken as parables for the vulgar, in the same way as the anthropomorphic passages relating to God, fails for the elementary reason that the parallel drawn is not a true parallel. The anthropomorphic passages are 'susceptible of esoteric interpretation according to the Arab usage in regard to metaphor,' whereas the descriptions of heaven and hell transcend the limit of legitimate allegorisation; to treat them as mere symbols is to suggest that the Prophet deliberately falsified the truth for the benefit of mankind, and 'the office of prophecy is far too sacred for that.'[12] The clinching proof of a physical resurrection, as al-Ghazālī sees the matter, is that God is admittedly omnipotent, and so it is clearly within His power to reconstitute the body and to effect a reunion between it and the soul, however much reason may boggle at such an idea. The issue is closely linked up with the problem of creation. It is intellectually feasible to accept three propositions: (1) that God existed without any world, (2) that God then created the world in the order we see all around us, (3) that God will in some future time produce a new order, namely that promised in Paradise. Thereafter everything could be annihilated, so that naught remains but Almighty God;[13] that is quite possible, except that the Koran explicitly states that the reward and punishment, heaven and hell, shall have no end.[14] Once accept the thesis that the world was created by God in time—and this has been proved at the beginning of the book—and there is no difficulty in believing in the resurrection of the body.[15]

Having satisfied his conscience with this sort of reasoning, al-Ghazālī felt himself free to conclude his masterpiece of ascetic theology, the *Iḥyā' 'ulūm al-dīn*, with a highly rhetorical account of the last days extensively plagiarised from the *Kitāb al-Tawahhum* of al-Muḥāsibī.[16] How comforting it must have been for him, and for so many faithful souls troubled by philosophical arguments which they could not understand, to sweep into oblivion all that high talk about union with the Active Intellect and to return in simple trust to God's plain words in the Koran! It was in the same mood of unquestioning faith that he ended his *Kīmiyā-yi sa'ādat*, that beautiful Persian summary of the *Iḥyā'*, by recapitulating once more the traditional story of the events after death. Here he advances as final proof a series of those popular anecdotes in which the hero of the story, usually a saint, is accorded in sleep an anticipatory peep into the next world. A typical instance is what befell 'Utba al-Ghulām.[17] He saw in a dream a beautiful houri out of Paradise who said to him, 'O 'Utba, I am in love with you. Beware lest you do anything so that I cannot come to you, and they hold me back from you!' 'Utba replied, 'I have triply divorced this world and will not go around after it any more, so that I may come to you.'[18] Those are the depths to which al-Ghazālī sunk, or the heights to which he rose, in the last phase of his long struggle to discover the truth.

It is significant that after Avicenna, eastern Islam produced no more great philosophers. The reaction against Greek learning, part as it seems of the wider political and theological struggle between orthodoxy and the Shī'a, reached its culmination in the educational programme of Niẓām al-Mulk and the subsequent revival of the study of *Ḥadīth* and *Kalām*. An attractive side-light on these cataclysmic events is thrown by the sharp and witty epigrams of a contemporary and countryman of al-Ghazālī, a shining star of that galaxy of geniuses rising in the skies of north-eastern Persia, the immortal Omar Khayyám. I have attempted elsewhere to show how Edward FitzGerald's favourite Persian fitted into the intellectual pattern of his times,[19] and mention him now only to call attention once more to the place he occupied in the contest between revelation and reason.[20]

> The secrets of the world, as we
> Succinctly on our tablets write,
> Are not expedient to recite:
> A plague to heart and head they be.
>
> Since there is none, as I can find,
> Of those brave wizards of to-day
> Worthy to hear, I cannot say
> The wondrous thoughts I have in mind.

The defeated philosopher's final recourse was therefore to silence. The Greek tradition, that had contributed so much to the formation of Moslem culture, now had to go underground in that very land which had given birth to its most brilliant Arabic exponents. The battle was over in the east. Thenceforward the future belonged to revelation, whether allied to scholastic theology of the Ash'arī pattern, or fundamentalism after the manner of the Ḥanbalīs, or the dogmatic speculations of the Shī'a, or that strange theosophy which Ibn 'Arabī (d. 638/1240) was presently to introduce. In the realms of poetry and art wonderful things were yet to be accomplished; in the book of abstract thought no more significant pages were written.

Philosophy still enjoyed a brief Indian summer in Islam's far west. It was fortunate for the development of mediaeval thought that Ibn Ḥazm (d. 456/1064), that fluent and conceited controversialist, should have been condemned during his lifetime as a heretic, and his writings proscribed;[21] had his advocacy of the narrow Ẓāhirī attitude to reason won the day, it is difficult to see how the brilliant Spanish school of Avempace (d. 533/1138), Ibn Ṭufail (d. 581/1185) and Averroes (d. 595/1198) could ever have flourished. Whereas Ibn Ṭufail has been famed in Europe since the seventeeth century, and his philosophical allegory *Living the Son of Wakeful*, with its defence of reason as an equal partner with revelation in the quest for truth, has enjoyed a wide circulation following Simon Ockley's elegant version,[22] Avempace and Averroes have had to wait until our own days to be methodically expounded.[23] Much research still remains to be done before the whole story of this last phase of Greek influence on Moslem thought can be fully told; meanwhile we have good cause to be thankful for the patient explorations of such eminent scholars as Palacios, Horten, Gauthier, Bouyges, and finally Van den Bergh whose recent translation of the *Incoherence of the Incoherence* is a massive contribution to this branch of learning.

Undaunted by al-Ghazālī's withering attack on the champions of pure reason, Averroes raised again the standard once carried aloft by the strong hands of al-Fārābī and Avicenna, and answered their critic's elaborate arguments point by point. In contrast to his adversary's polemical preface, he opens his reply briefly and with a cool and dignified concision. 'The aim of this book is to show the different degrees of assent and conviction attained by the assertions in *The Incoherence of the Philosophers*, and to prove that the greater part has not reached the degree of evidence and of truth.'[24] While the *Tahāfut al-Tahāfut* in the nature of things is largely an exercise—and what an exercise!—

in construction by destruction, in the *Faṣl al-maqāl* Averroes attempts briefly, and for the last time in mediaeval Islam, to make the peace between revelation and reason. Here he restates the case, which had been pleaded from the beginning, for accepting the truth even when first enunciated by infidels; in his exposition of 'rational syllogism' he echoes al-Kindī's innocent delight of discovery.

'It is difficult, if not impossible, for a single man by himself and on his own initiative to light upon all that he needs in this connexion, just as it is difficult for one man to elucidate all that he requires to know with regard to the varieties of legal syllogism;[25] indeed this is even more the case with reference to knowledge of the rational syllogism. So if someone else has already enquired into this matter, it is clear that we ought to look at what our predecessor has said to help us in our own undertaking, alike whether that previous investigator was of the same religion as ourselves or not. For in regard to the instrument by which our reasoning is precisely refined it is immaterial to consider, touching its property of refining, whether that instrument was invented by a co-religionist of ours or by one who did not share our faith; the only proviso is that it fulfils the condition of being sound and efficacious. (In using the expression "one who did not share our faith" I refer to those speculators who looked into these things before the coming of Islam.) This being the case, since all that needs to be done in the investigation of rational syllogisms has already been explored perfectly by the ancients, all that would seem to be necessary for us to do is to take their writings into our hands and to study what they have said on the subject. If that is all correct, then we will accept it from them; if there is anything incorrect in what they have written, we will call attention to such deficiencies.'[26]

Averroes was of course by no means original in pinning his faith to logic as the sovereign recipe for the discovery of truth; al-Fārābī before him had made the same observation,[27] and it is common knowledge that logic exercised a powerful fascination in Islam; al-Ghazālī even attempted to derive the forms of syllogistic reasoning from the Koran.[28] Averroes, coming at the end of a long chapter, was bold enough to claim that 'Divine ordinance itself requires us to look into the books of the ancients, since their intention and goal in what they wrote was the same goal as that towards which Divine ordinance has urged us'; and he added, 'Any man forbidding the study of these books to anyone properly qualified to look into them—anyone, that is, who combines sagacity of spirit with religious uprightness and moral virtue—thereby bars mankind from the very door whereby Divine ordinance calls men to get to know God, the door of speculation leading to the true knowledge of Him.... The fact that this or that man has gone astray or stumbled through studying those books, whether on account of some constitutional defect, or because his study of them was badly organised, or that his passions dominated him, or owing to the fact that he did not find a teacher to direct him to the understanding of their contents, or as a result of the combination of all or some of these causes—this fact does not oblige you to bar those properly qualified from examining them.'[29]

'Those properly qualified'—that was the heart of the matter. Averroes agreed with his Moslem forerunners in preaching 'one truth for the masses, and another for the elect.' The three classes of proof—demonstrative, dialectical and rhetorical[30]—should be kept carefully apart and used strictly on the three classes of men to whom they were appropriate. The mistake made by the Mu'tazilites, and even by the Ash'arites, was to expose to a too advanced method of Koranic exegesis those who were not ready for such high adventures, and that was the true cause of the bitter quarrels and dangerous hatreds which had torn Islam to pieces. The Koran itself contained all the varieties of argument needed to bring all sorts and conditions of men to salvation; when properly studied and applied, philosophy was 'the friend, indeed the foster-sister of religion.'[31] All this was smooth and reasonable talk indeed; face to face with such an eloquent defence of revelation, even if reason was called in as an equal ally, one might well be at a loss to understand why Averroes should have been condemned as an out-and-out free-thinker, and how his far from extremist teaching so mysteriously misled into heresy its Christian exponents in the thirteenth century.[32] But the time was past when men would acquiesce in putting reason on the same level as revelation. St. Thomas Aquinas for Christianity, reverting to St. Augustine's 'Therefore seek not to understand that thou mayest believe, but believe that thou mayest understand,'[33] was to argue, 'I know by reason that something is true because *I see* that it is true; but I believe that something is true because *God has said it*. In those two cases the cause of my assent is specifically different, consequently science and faith should be held as two specifically different kinds of assent.'[34] As for Islam, the sweet reason of Averroes' patient voice would be silenced by the thunder of Ibn Taimīya's uncompromising denunciation. By the time the illustrious Ibn Khaldūn (d. 808/1406) came to draw up his catalogue of the sacred and profane sciences, philosophy had fallen so far from grace as to be relegated to a string of contemptuous paragraphs following the discussion of magic, talismans and alchemy, and to share with astrology the signal honour of his summary refutation.[35]

So far we have largely considered the problem of reason and revelation as though acceptance of the message of the Koran and of the findings of Greek philosophy were for the Moslem the only two possible approaches to a tranquil faith. We have seen how the construction of a creed out of the 'plain language' of the Scriptures, like the development of a political theory and a legal system, had called for interpretation of God's words, and the enlargement of their area of application by use of the reputed sayings of Mohammed. The Mu'tazilites had brought in methods of dialectical reasoning, derived through the Christian fathers from the pagan Greeks, to organise their theology and defend it against attack from within and without Islam; the Ash'arites had been pleased to take over their methods, while rejecting their conclusions. But all this failed to hush the nagging whisper of doubt; men differed in their exegesis of the Divine proclamation, and a hundred sects and schisms vociferously claimed equal right to be considered orthodox. Was there not some third way to the truth, a way which would surmount all obstacles of uncertainty? Was there not to be found a beacon fire, like the burning bush that led Moses in the wilderness,[36] which would cast over the whole of life's dark path the guiding light of infallible authority? The mystics, as we have suggested briefly before and will expound at greater length hereafter, offered personal communion with God as the answer to this perplexing problem; a particular sect of the Shī'a had an alternative solution to propose.

The Ismā'īlī answer to the anxious mind's questionings was peculiarly ingenious; for a considerable length of time and over a considerable extent of territory it prevailed, until the catastrophic events of the twelfth century tumbled the Fāṭimids from their high Egyptian throne and sent their survivors scurrying for refuge to the mountains of Yemen, and finally to distant India. Like most if not all Islamic religious movements, Ismā'īlism combined politics with theology; it shared with the rest of the Shī'a in working for the overthrow of the usurping caliphate and its replacement by the family of 'Alī. Now 'Alī was believed by his partisans to have been privy to all the esoteric teachings of the Koran and the Prophet; his position vis-à-vis Mohammed was the same as that of Abel to Adam, Shem to Noah, Ishmael to Abraham, Aaron to Moses, and Simon Peter to Christ.[37] His successors were the unique repositories of this secret doctrine, which was by definition certain and authoritative; in times of persecution it gave those who embraced it a cause to conspire and to die for, while in the happier days of rulership it hallowed strict obedience to lawful government with the halo of righteousness. ' 'Alī is the gate to religion; whoever enters that gate is a believer, and whoever departs from it is an infidel.'[38] By means of this and similar pronouncements attributed to the founder of the faith, validity was secured for a theocratic regime that has attracted the most widely divergent judgments. 'Ismā'īlism,' writes Ivanow, 'beyond any doubt, was chiefly based on, and animated by fervent religious sentiment, without which it could have never come into existence:— in the "negative" version it appears as a doctrine of atheism. It was, also quite undoubtedly, one of the most consistent monotheistic systems ever conceived by human mind:—the "negative" version declares that it was really a doctrine of dualism, the "religion of the Magians". The central and fundamental ideal of Ismā'īlism, also common to various Shī'ite sects, was the ultimate triumph of Islam as the sole religion of the world, the ultimate union of mankind in "one flock under one shepherd", i.e. the Imam from the house of the Prophet, who alone can guide long suffering humanity to a righteous and peaceful life, filling the earth with justice and equity even as much as it has always been filled with injustice, oppression, and bestiality:—in the "negative" version we find that Ismā'īlism was "invented to blow up Islam from the inside". In the Shī'ite doctrine the 'Alid descent of the Imam was one of the primary and indispensable dogmas:— the "negative" version "proves" that al-Mahdī and his successors were the descendants of a Persian heresiarch, or a Jew.'[39]

Thanks to the laborious and patient investigations of a group of able scholars—Massignon, Ivanow, Kraus, Strothmann, Fyzee, Ḥusain Kāmil, Lewis and Corbin are prominent among them[40]—we now have a vastly better informed and more accurate knowledge of the history and literature of the Ismā'īlīs than would have appeared possible thirty years ago. The bibliography of the subject has meanwhile grown to such proportions that even a cursory review would provide abundant material for a course of lectures; for our present purpose it is proposed to give a brief account of the contents of one recently published Ismā'īlī book which illustrates aptly the strenuous effort made by this sect to resolve the problem with which we have concerned ourselves. This work, the *Kitāb Jāmi' al-ḥikmatain* of Nāṣir-i Khusrau, is appropriately sub-titled by its French editor, Henry Corbin, 'Harmonie de la philosophie grecque et de la théosophie ismaélienne.'[41] Nāṣir-i Khusrau, who was born near Balkh—another product of north-eastern Persia—in 394/1004 and died between 465/1072 and 470/1077,[42] has long been famous as a poet, and author of a most interesting travelogue;[43] his Ismā'īlī writings in fluent Persian prose, publication of which was begun shortly after the first world-war,[44] have in recent times following successive discoveries proved him to be perhaps the most fertile and certainly the most lucid exponent of that sect, to which he became finally converted during his six-years' visit to Fāṭimid Egypt ending in 444/1052.[45] The *Jāmi' al-ḥikmatain* was composed in 462/1069, and thus represents the author's maturest and most completely finalised views.[46]

The form in which this work is cast is certainly curious; it takes the shape of an elaborate commentary on an Ismā'īlī poem composed by a certain Abu 'l-Haitham al-Jurjānī, and it was written at the request of 'Alī ibn Asad, Prince of Badakhshan, whose family claimed descent from Alexander the Great.[47] The poem, the text of which is first reproduced at length[48] and subsequently discussed piecemeal, propounds in 82 couplets a series of questions on a variety of somewhat obscure problems, the answers to which Nāsir-i Khusrau essays to offer. He is quite frank in his approach to the task: 'Since those so-called scholars have denounced as infidels those who know the science of created things, the seekers after the how and why have become silent, and the expounders of this science have also remained mute, so that ignorance has overmastered all the people, especially the inhabitants of our land of Khorasan and the territories of the east.... No one has written a book on the how and why of creation, because out of the five causes which we have shown above to be necessary to the production of any book first the seeker after this knowledge, who is the final cause, has ceased to exist, and secondly the expounder of this knowledge, who is the efficient cause, has also passed away; and with the disappearance of these two causes from among the people of this land, the science of religion itself has vanished. In the afore-mentioned land nobody now remains who is capable of uniting the science of true religion, which is a product of the Holy Ghost, with the science of creation, which is an appendage of philosophy. For the philosopher relegates these so-called scholars to the rank of the beasts, and on account of their ignorance despises the religion of Islam; while these so-called scholars declare the philosopher to be an infidel. As a result, neither true religion nor philosophy remains any more in this land.'[49] This is the lamentable situation he hopes to remedy, having in mind two distinct audiences. 'In this book I have addressed the wise men of religion with quotations from God's Book and the Traditions of the Prophet, while for the wise men of philosophy and those learned in logic I have provided rational demonstrations accompanied by conclusive and satisfying premisses. For the treasury of wisdom is the mind of the Seal of the inheritors of the prophets, but some fragrance of that wisdom is also contained in the books of the ancients.'[50]

Some of the problems set by Abu 'l-Haitham have, as might be expected, a typically mediaeval ring. Thus, verse 60 propounds a hoary enigma:

'Who can indicate precisely where a circle
starts and ends?
Which came first, the egg or chicken?
That's a baffling one, my friends.'

This is how Nāsir-i Khusrau solves the riddle. 'If anyone describes a circle, and then asks someone else to say where he began to draw it, his question will be idle. For supposing someone points to a spot and says, "That is where you began to draw the circle," the first man can always reply, "Produce some proof of your assertion that the drawing started here," which the other man will counter with, "And you produce some proof that it did not start here." As neither of the two is able to furnish any rational proof in support of his own claim and in refutation of the other's statement, it is clear that the question is entirely futile. Yet reason acknowledges that the circumference did have a beginning and an end. To say however that it is ridiculous to discuss which came first, the egg or the chicken, is not allowed by philosophers; that is how the man-in-the-street talks, for he thinks that just as a chicken comes only from an egg, so an egg comes only from a chicken. Now the real answer to this question is as follows. The egg is a potential bird, and if it is completely reared by the bird it will emerge out of potentiality into actuality. If there is no bird to bring it to actuality, the egg will never become a chicken but will go to waste. So we recognise that if the egg had come first, and no bird existed to bring it to actuality, no bird would ever have come out of that egg. Since the bird was necessary in order to bring that primal egg to actuality, then that bird existed before that egg, and itself fashioned that egg. Here is a second proof that the chicken came before the egg. The bird's egg is a thing fabricated with shape and design; there are within it various objects all set one inside the other, while a thin shell wraps the whole around and is itself contained in a hard shell that has no holes or fissures whatsoever. So we realise that it is the product of a maker possessed of knowledge. It is of its nature to make things in certain ways; for it is reasonable to assume that any body is shaped according to the purpose and design of its maker. So the bird's egg, by token of the marks of fabrication patent upon it, is a fabricated thing. Moreover it requires a bird in order to emerge out of the potentiality that is in it into actuality, while the bird has no need of it. Therefore it is absurd to say that the bird, which has no need of the egg, is a fabrication of that egg which itself requires the bird. Hence reason testifies that the producer of the egg is the bird, while the egg is the bird's product; and no product can be its own producer. So we have established that the chicken came before the egg; in the same way the date-seed came before the date-tree, and the animal came before the sperm that issues from it. For just as the egg will never become a bird without a bird to rear it, so the sperm of an animal will never become an animal without an animal to nurture it; so if it were allowed that the sperm could exist before the animal, it would also be allowable that the egg existed before the bird. Now since animals to-day come into being by birth, and those individuals who existed before this themselves had begetters, it follows necessarily that there was once a beginning to birth, in order for it to come to pass to-day; for that which has no beginning cannot come to pass at all. Therefore as we see by the arbitrament of reason that birth takes place to-day, and that our child who is as yet unborn will itself come into being as a result of birth, it must result that there was once a beginning to birth. Since there must have been a beginning to birth, it is established that there was once a begetter that was itself not born, and whose being was without birth. . . . We say moreover that the origin of every plant, such as wheat and barley, and likewise trees came about in the same way. If anyone should say, "The seed is to the plant and the tree as the egg is to the bird, and the sperm to the animal, because just as the egg comes from the bird so too the seed comes from the tree; therefore it follows that the date-tree existed first so that the seed was produced from it, and the green corn existed first so that the wheat was produced from it," our answer would be as follows:—"This is a false analogy; on the contrary, the date-seed came before the date-tree, and the wheat-grain came before the green corn. The original thing is the seed, not the plant; the plant is to the seed just as the egg is to the bird, and the sperm to the animal, contrary to what you say." The proof of the correctness of this assertion is that the seed is an imperfect plant, while no one can say that the plant is an imperfect seed.... The seeds are the original pairs, and the birth of every tree derives from the first pair that came together. So we realise that the date-tree was born of male and female, and the seed of that tree came together in one place. Similarly every species of plant stands in the same relationship as does man to Adam and Eve, and every variety of horse to the original pair of horses, and all the kingdoms of nature to heaven and earth. Nothing exists that has not come into being out of a pair that existed before it. In the same way the soul and the intellect spring from the primal pair which existed before all beings, while the world—namely our second heaven and earth—was born of the primal heaven and earth, as we have stated before. Therefore by these demonstrative arguments we state that the chicken came first, and then the egg. Q.E.D.'[51]

That is a not unfair specimen of Nāsir-i Khusrau's scholastic method of exposition. But naturally he also deals with matters of weightier moment; he is ambitious to gather within his comparatively narrow compass all the mysteries of creation. The whole world of being is for him, as for every Ismā'īlī, one gigantic and infinitely involved symbol.[52] The principle of esoteric interpretation (*ta'wīl*), which is made to signify 'bringing things back to their primary significance,'[53] applies not only to the exegesis of the Koran but to the unrolling of the entire scroll of nature. Take a little physiological curiosity which might at first thought be considered to possess no inner meaning:[54]

'Why is it, when boys are born they keep an upright head,
Whereas girls contrariwise hang upside down instead?'

The natural scientists offer as the explanation the fact that the male temperament is warm and dry, while the female is cold and moist; girls are therefore top-heavy, and when they turn in the womb their heads automatically swing downwards. But this interpretation is merely superficial; the Imams (*ahl-i ta'yīd*) go much deeper. 'The female nature is weak, like the exoteric aspect of the Book and the Law; and everyone who is attached to the exoteric aspect of the Book and the Law is weak of soul.' Literalists (*ẓāhiriyān*) are like the women mentioned in Koran II 223:

> Your women are a tillage for you; so come
> unto your tillage as you wish.

Allegorical interpreters (*ahl-i ta'wīl*) see in this verse a reference to those who answer the call of the missionary (*dā'ī*), who brings them to the truth. Esoterists (*ahl-i bāṭin*) are like men; the real man was the Prophet sent by God to all people, who are in the status of women in relation to him. As in law women have the duty of obeying their men, and people have the duty of obeying the Prophet, it is clear that the Prophet is a man, and that the people are all in the position of a woman in relation to this man. A further proof of this profound truth is provided by Koran IV 38, which in its primary signification refers to disobedient wives:

> And those you fear may be rebellious
> admonish; banish them to their couches,
> and beat them. If they then obey you,
> look not for any way against them.

The Prophet is commanded by God here, following the inward meaning, to treat polytheists in the same way, as also in Koran IV 66:

> So turn away from them, and admonish them,
> and say to them penetrating words
> about themselves.

Further confirmation is furnished by Koran II 189:

Fight them, till there is no persecution
and the religion is God's; then if they
give over, there shall be no enmity
save for evildoers.

Similarly the Divine ordinance assigning to men twice the inheritance of women points to the fact that he who possesses both the inward and the outward aspects of the Law is a true *man* of religion, while the one who knows only the exoteric interpretation and not the esoteric is a *woman* of religion. The woman child is born turning the back on the inward aspect of the faith, while the man child turns his face towards the true knowledge.

After this ingenious exercise it is no surprise to find that the great facts of the universe are in reality symbols of wonderful Ismā'īlī mysteries. The sun occupies in the macrocosm which is the physical world the same position as the heart in the microcosm which is man; the moon is the brain; the five planets are the five senses. 'Since man is corporeally the child of the macrocosm, and spiritually the child of the Universal Soul, it follows that the macrocosm is as it were the body of the Universal Soul, having the instruments we have mentioned. It was in this sense that Jesus the son of Mary—upon him be peace—said, "I go unto my father, and my father is in heaven";[55] that is, "My particular soul is returning to the Universal Soul which is in heaven." The ignorant ones of his community thought that he said, "I am the son of God." '[56] The Divine warrant for this correspondence between the macrocosm and the microcosm is to be found in Koran XLI 53:

We shall show to them Our signs in the horizons and
in themselves, till it is clear to them
that it is the truth.

The fact that we have two eyes, two ears, two nostrils, two organs of taste,[57] and two hands proves that we are made up of two parts, just as the heavenly sphere is said to consist of two parts. One half of us is to the left and one to the right, while a straight line runs down our middle, beginning with the parting of the hair and so proceeding through the whole body; that corresponds with the equator that divides the signs of the Zodiac. Thus we have five senses, and ten instruments of sense; similarly there are five planets, and ten 'houses' of the planets. Finally the human spirit resides in the heart, and the rational soul lodges in the brain, the five senses being at the service of this pair of rulers; in the macrocosm the sun and the moon possess only one 'house' each, and rule over the five planets.[58] But that is not the end of the matter. Just as God created the human body in the similitude of the universe, so the Prophet organised the true religion in the same way. In the 'world of religion' the Prophet is the life-giving sun, or the heart; the Prophet's Executor (*waṣī*, *sc.* 'Ali) is the moon controlling the good order and welfare of the faith, or the brain; each of these two lodges in one 'house' only, the Prophet's 'house' being the composition of the Book and the Law without its interpretation, while the Executor's 'house' is the interpretation of the Book and the Law without its actual revelation. The five planets of the faith are the five grades of Imām, Bāb, Ḥujja, Dā'ī and Ma'dhūn; the two 'houses' occupied by each of these are the exoteric and esoteric interpretation of the Book and the Law.[59]

The Ismā'īlīs, like the philosophers, were delighted to accept as genuine the saying attributed to Mohammed that the first thing created by God was the intellect.[60] This gave scope for a further series of easy parallels. The Universal Intellect is the same as the Pen mentioned in the Koran;[61] the Universal Soul is the Tablet;[62] the physical world is as it were God's written book. With these clues to help us, we are able to reach a better understanding of Koran LII 1–6:

By the Mount
and a Book inscribed
in a parchment unrolled,

by the House inhabited
and the roof uplifted
and the sea swarming.

'The "Mount" is the Universal Body, which is like a great mountain; indeed, this is the Universal Mountain. The "Book inscribed" is the forms and shapes that are written on this body. The "parchment unrolled" is the air in which this "inscribed Book" turns. The "House inhabited" is the world, which is a tent without any opening, like an inhabited house that has no cracks or fissures. The "roof uplifted" is the upraised heaven. The "sea swarming" is infinite space, that may be thought of as extending infinitely outside the tent of the skies.'[63]

So much for the material universe. 'In the world of religion, the Prophet is also the Pen of God; the noble Koran is God's Book inscribed by the Pen—that is, the Prophet—upon the Tablet, i.e. the Executor. Just as we would never have known the primal Book except through the Tablet, so without the Executor we would never have known the Koran. The rational proof of the fact that the creation of the world in corporeal substance is God's primal Book, and that the Koran is His second Book, is to be found in Koran II 1:

Alif Lam Mim
That is the Book, wherein is no doubt,
a guidance to the godfearing.

Alif here means length, *lām* means breadth, and *mīm* means depth; the reference is to the world, which possesses length, breadth and depth. Moreover God says, "That is the Book, wherein is no doubt"; that is, it is manifest that it was made by God, and it is "a guidance to the godfearing." If by this Book God had meant the Koran, He would have said "This is the Book," because this verse is at the head of the Book. Since God said "That is the Book," and not "This is the Book," this hint is proof to men of reason that by these words God intends not the Koran but the world of creation. Therefore the visible Book (the world of creation) and the audible Book (the noble Koran) are two writings of God's executed by two Pens upon two Tablets for the benefit of men having a share of understanding.'[64]

Nāṣir-i Khusrau explores all the orders of created beings; his angelology is of especial interest. Abu 'l-Haitham in verses 14–15 of his poem had appealed urgently for information:

> 'There are angels, there are fairies, there are demons too, I know;
> Absolutely they exist, and I repeat that that is so.
> Tell me what and how they are, and fortify with proofs your tale,
> If you can discreetly extricate this topic from its veil.'

His Ismā'īlī commentator was fully equal to the occasion. The rational answer of philosophy, he tells us, is that the angels are the heavenly bodies, which possess both life and speech.[65] Thābit ibn Qurra,[66] 'he who translated the books of philosophy out of the Greek language and script into the Arabic language and script', argued that the spheres and the stars were alive and vocal by pointing out that their bodies were certainly as noble and subtle as those of men, who are endowed with these faculties. As for fairies, the philosophers know nothing of them; however, they do believe in demons, which they say are the disembodied spirits of ignorant and wicked men. They cannot leave their former physical surroundings; in particular they haunt deserts and lure travellers to destruction.[67] That is the substance of what Rhazes says in his *Fī 'l-'ilm al-ilāhī*;[68] he states that these demons make themselves out to be angels sent by God to certain men bearing the mandate of prophecy, and as a result vast confusion is provoked and great slaughter ensues.[69] Nāṣir-i Khusrau remarks that he has already refuted 'that impudent madman' in his *Bustān al-'uqūl*,[70] and will therefore not take up time on this occasion to repeat the process.

That, then, is how the philosophers would solve Abu 'l-Haitham's problem. The Imams, resting on the dual authority of the Prophet and the Executor, have their own explanation to offer. The angels are pure souls, an original creation of God, five in number—Reason, Spirit, Fortune, Victory and Vision;[71] their exoteric names are the Pen, the Tablet, Seraphiel, Michael and Gabriel. Of these originated beings two, Reason and Spirit, are the roots, while Fortune, Victory and Vision are the branches. In the physical universe the two roots are the stars and the spheres; the three branches are the mineral, vegetable and animal kingdoms. In the microcosm of religion the two roots are the Prophet and the Executor; the three branches are the Imām, the Ḥujja and the Dā'ī. Just as the stars—the visible angels—are intermediaries between the actual 'originated' angels and the potential angels who are men, so the Prophets, Executors and Imams are intermediaries between the potential and the actual angels, their function being by means of the Book and the Law to make men actual angels. 'Whoever is able to convert a potential angel into an actual angel has already attained the rank of angelhood; he is God's viceroy in the earth.'[72] This is the meaning of Koran XLIII 60:

> Had We willed, We would have appointed angels among you to be successors in the earth.

As for the fairies, they are to be equated with the jinn whose purpose, like that of men, is to serve God:[73]

> I have not created jinn and mankind except to serve Me.

The demons were formerly fairies, but they fell from grace in the manner recounted in Koran XVIII 48:

> And when We said to the angels, 'Bow
> yourselves to Adam'; so they bowed
> themselves, save Iblis; he was one of
> the jinn, and committed ungodliness
> against his Lord's command.

Fairies become angels by obeying God, and demons by disobeying Him; the intermediary between them and God is the Prophet, who is sent to fairies and men alike as Koran LXXII 1–2 proves:

> Say: 'It has been revealed to me that a
> company of the jinn gave ear, then they
> said, "We have indeed heard a Koran
> wonderful,
> guiding to rectitude."'

Further confirmation is furnished by Koran XLVI 28:

> And when We turned to thee a company of jinn
> giving ear to the Koran, and when they were
> in its presence they said, 'Be silent!'
> Then, when it was finished, they turned back
> to their people, warning.

In the world of religion men are divided into two classes, fairy and human. Fairies (or jinn—the Arabic word means 'covered')—are invisible to the common run of men. From this it follows that in Mohammed's community there is a class of 'fairy' men who are unseen, namely the potential angels, and a class of 'human' men who are visible, to wit the potential fairies; the fairies may by obedience also become angels, but by disobedience both fairies and humans may turn into demons. This division corresponds with the 'exoterics' and the 'esoterics'. 'It is the rational soul in every man that is the potential angel, and the potential angel is a fairy, as we have said. The appetitive and passionate souls in every person are a pair of potential demons. Every man whose rational soul brings his passionate and appetitive souls to obedience becomes an angel; every man whose passionate and appetitive souls control his rational soul becomes an actual demon. This was what the Prophet meant when he said, "Every man has two Satans that beguile him." He was asked, "O Prophet, do you also have these two demons?" He replied, "I had two Satans, but God succoured me against them and they surrendered." We have therefore made it clear that in every man there is an angel and a demon, while he himself is a fairy. The demon was not created by God, but owes its existence to man's disobedience. Fairies are potential angels, and become actual angels by obedience; they also become actual demons by disobedience. Men are thus potential angels and potential demons; and the other world is full of actual angels and actual demons.'[74]

This is as good a scene as any with which to end our casual glance at the strange and bewildering diorama of Ismā'īlī speculation. It is a montage made up of genuine stills from Greek philosophy and science, stuck together with trick shots manufactured in oriental studios bearing the outlandish names of Gnosticism, Hermetism and Manicheism, the whole reel being fitted with a sound-track made up of apt quotations from the Arabic Koran. For those who had a taste for mystery, Ismā'īlism was surely the mystery-religion *in excelsis;* the wonder is that with it should have been associated a statecraft so masterful, and a culture so varied and attractive. But that statecraft was doomed to bankruptcy, that culture proved to possess the fertility of the streptococcus; Ismā'īlism was dying of a monstrous cancer, even before the surgeon's knife of outraged orthodoxy struck it to the heart. Avicenna in his childhood had heard more than enough of the high-sounding Fāṭimid rhetoric which so completely enraptured Nāṣir-i Khusrau's poetic soul. 'My father,' he tells us in his autobiography, 'was one of those who had responded to the Egyptian propagandist (who was an Ismā'īlī); he, and my brother too, had listened to what they had to say about the Spirit and the Intellect, after the fashion in which they preach and understand the matter. They would therefore discuss these things together, while I listened and comprehended all that they said; but my spirit would not assent to their argument.'[75] Well might the Persian Plato revolt against such a prostitution of human reason in the name of infallible authority; it is one of the ironies of history that it should have been the same al-Ghazālī who did most to drive Ismā'īlism along with philosophy out of the fold of orthodox Islam.[76]

NOTES

[1] Especially in his *Maqāṣid al-falāsifa* in which he attempted to summarise the main tendencies of Greek philosophy.

[2] *Tahāfut al-falāsifa*, now newly edited by Sulaimān Dunyā.

[3] *Op. cit.*, p. 32.

[4] *Ibid.*, pp. 35-6.

[5] A leading point of discussion between the Mu'tazilites and the orthodox theologians.

[6] *Op. cit.*, pp. 313–15.

[7] *Ibid.*, p. 282.

[8] *Ibid.*, p. 288.

[9] This somewhat sophistical argument is repeated by Khwāja-zāda Brusawī (d. 893/1488) in his *Tahāfut al-falāsifa* (Cairo, 1302/1885), pp. 132–3.

[10] Koran xxxii 17.

[11] A well-known *ḥadīth*, derived from 1 *Cor.* 2: 9.

[12] *Op. cit.*, p. 299.

[13] Koran xxviii 88.

[14] In passages too numerous to cite; cf. ii 23, 37, 75, 76, 157 etc.

[15] *Op. cit.*, p. 312.

[16] See above, p. 43.

[17] See L. Massignon, *Essai sur les origines*, p. 145, n.2.

[18] *Op. cit.* (Teheran, 1320/1941), p. 997.

[19] In my *Omar Khayyám: a New Version.*

[20] No. 206 in the Cambridge MS.

[21] See C. van Arendonk in *Encyclopaedia of Islam*, ii, p. 386.

[22] First published in 1708.

[23] A good bibliography for Avempace is contained in E. Rosenthal, 'The Place of Politics in the Philosophy of Ibn Bajja' in *Islamic Culture*, xxv 1.

[24] S. van den Bergh, *Averroes' Tahafut al-Tahafut*, i, p. 1.

[25] Using the term *qiyās* here in its connotation in jurisprudence.

[26] Averroes, *Faṣl al-maqāl* (ed. L. Gauthier), pp. 3–4.

[27] See *al-Tanbīh 'alā sabīl al-sa'āda*, pp. 21–24.

[28] In his *al-Qusṭās al-mustaqīm*.

[29] *Faṣl al-maqāl*, pp. 6–7.

[30] *Ibid.*, p. 26.

[31] *Ibid.*, p. 32.

[32] See especially L. Gauthier, *La théorie d'Ibn Rochd.*

33 Aquinas, *On the Gospel of St. John*, xxix 6.
34 E. Gilson, *Reason and Revelation in the Middle Ages*, p. 73.
35 See Ibn Khaldûn, *Muqaddima*.
36 Koran xx 9–10.
37 See M. Kāmil Ḥusain, *Diwān al-Mu'aiyad* (Cairo, 1949), p. 72.
38 *Ibid.*, p. 84.
39 W. Ivanow, *The Rise of the Fatimids*, pp. xvi–xvii.
40 The bibliography of Ismā'īlī studies has now grown to such proportions that its exposition would fill many pages. The publication of specialist bibliographies would be a signal help to the advancement of all branches of Islamic research.
41 Published at Teheran in 1953, the joint-editor being Mohammed Mo'in.
42 See H. Corbin, *op. cit.*, p. 36.
43 The *Safar-nāma*, edited and translated by C. Schefer, Paris, 1881; English translation (partial) by G. Le Strange, London, 1888; new edition of the Persian text, Berlin, 1923.
44 Commencing with the *Zād al-musāfirīn*, Berlin, 1923. See further E. Berthels in *Encyclopaedia of Islam*, ii, p. 870.
45 H. Corbin, *op. cit.*, pp. 28–33.
46 W. Ivanow, deceived by the wrong date 422/1031, doubted the authenticity of the book, see his *Guide to Ismaili Literature*, p. 70. H. Corbin has proved its genuineness beyond reasonable doubt, see *op. cit.*, pp. 39–44.
47 H. Corbin, *op. cit.*, p. 47.
48 *Ibid.*, text, pp. 19–30.
49 *Ibid.*, pp. 15–16.
50 *Ibid.*, p. 18.
51 *Ibid.*, pp. 264–7.
52 For the Ismā'īlī doctrine of *mathal* and *mamthūl* see Kāmil Ḥusain, *op. cit.*, pp. 106–8.
53 See H. Corbin, *op. cit.*, pp. 67–68.
54 Verse 67, see *op. cit.*, pp. 295 ff.
55 Cf. *John* 14: 12, *Mat.* 16: 17.
56 *Op. cit.*, p. 282.
57 Sc. the mouth and the sexual organ.
58 *Op. cit.*, pp. 283–8.
59 *Ibid.*, pp. 290–1, cf. Introd. p. 89.
60 See J. W. Sweetman, *Islam and Christian Theology*, ii, p. 119.
61 *Ibid.*, cf. Koran lxviii 1.
62 Koran lxxxv 22.

[63] H. Corbin, *op. cit.*, p. 231.
[64] *Ibid.*, p. 232.
[65] J. W. Sweetman, *op. cit.*, ii, p. 78.
[66] See C. Brockelmann, *Geschichte der arabischen Litteratur*, i, p. 217; Suppl. i, 384–6.
[67] Like the jinn as represented in Arab legend.
[68] For this lost work, see above, p. 38.
[69] A remarkable interpretation of the early history of Islam!
[70] This work appears not to have survived.
[71] See H. Corbin, *op. cit.*, Introd., pp. 91–112.
[72] *Ibid.*, Text, p. 139.
[73] Koran li 56.
[74] H. Corbin, *op. cit.*, pp. 143–4.
[75] See A. J. Arberry, *Avicenna on Theology*, p. 9.
[76] Especially in his polemic *al-Mustaẓhirī fī faḍā'iḥ al-Bāṭinīya.*

IV

We have considered how theology, philosophy and infallible authority endeavoured variously to resolve the conflict within Islam between reason and revelation. In the individual quest after certainty all three of these approaches had its own especial guidance to offer, and many were satisfied to follow one or the other; far more were content with simple trust in God's message and the Prophet's example, dismissing as unlawful curiosity the mind's questions provoked by both. But there remained still a fourth way by which the earnest believer might hope to reach his journey's end, the way of spiritual discipline and, if might be, personal communion with the Creator. This was the mystic's path, in illustration of which we shall examine in particular the life and sayings of one man, an ecstatic famous in Islam for the boldness of his utterances and the patent authenticity of his experience.

Bistam was a fair-sized township in the Persian north-eastern region of Qumis, upon the highway to Nishapur; when Yāqūt the geographer visited the place on the eve of the Mongol invasion he found extensive markets there but no rich men's houses.[1] It lay in the shadow of high mountains, and a great river hard by supplied the inhabitants with water that possessed remarkable properties. If a visitor to the town who had passionate love in his heart drank of it, the passion passed away at once. It had a bitter flavour, and was highly beneficial to sufferers from halitosis; when applied as a clyster it was a sure remedy for haemorrhoids. The locality, which swarmed with small snakes and stinging flies, was famous for its rosy apples that were exported all the way to Iraq and sold there as Bistamis.

Ophthalmia was unknown in the place. Clustered on a hill overlooking the town were the ruins of a spacious palace said to have been built by the Sassanian monarch Shapur II (A.D. 310–379).[2] Finally we are told that the local hens would not eat human excrement.[3]

How much of the foregoing information is relevant to the career of Bistam's most famous citizen it is of course impossible to say; psychologists of the future may be able to explain his entire character by reference to one or another of the features of his early environment. Abū Yazīd Ṭaifūr ibn 'Īsā ibn Surūshān al-Bisṭāmī was born about the end of the 8th century; his grandfather Surūshān was a convert from Zoroastrianism to Islam.[4] Of his father 'Īsā we are told that after wedding Abū Yazīd's mother he abstained from consummating the marriage for forty nights for reasons of extreme scrupulosity. Abū Yazīd was the middle of three brothers, and he also had two sisters.[5] He is said to have attended no fewer than 313 teachers, the last of them being Ja'far ibn Muḥammad al-Ṣādiq (not to be confused with the Shī'ite imam Ja'far al-Ṣādiq)[6] whom he served as a *sāqī* for two years.[7] Among his early associates was Abū 'Alī al-Sindī[8] whom he taught 'the Ḳur'ān verses necessary for prayer,'[9] receiving in exchange instruction in 'the Divine Unity and the Realities.'[10] It has been suggested that this Abū 'Alī al-Sindī was an Indian,[11] and that 'it is not impossible that Indian influences may have affected Abū Yazīd through him.'[12] If there were substance in this conjecture it would be extremely important for the reconstruction of the history of mystical thought in Islam, for it would point to a very early connexion between Sufi speculation on union with God and the teachings of Patanjali.[13] Unfortunately there is nothing to confirm that Abū 'Alī in fact came from India; his place-name al-Sindī might it is true be derived from the province of Sind,[14] but it is to be noted that Sind was also the name of a village in Khorasan,[15] and that brings us much nearer home to Bistam. Considering moreover that the only certain information we have about

Abū 'Alī al-Sindī is Abū Yazīd's reported saying that he taught him 'the Divine Unity and the Realities,' it seems hazardous in the extreme to construct an elaborate theory of Vedanta origins for al-Bisṭāmī's mystical formation upon so slender a clue.

If the available details of Abū Yazīd's early life are meagre, what we know about his later years is not much more extensive. We are told that he was banished from Bistam seven times,[16] no doubt on account of the scandal to the orthodox caused by his ecstatic utterances. He is stated to have performed the Mecca pilgrimage forty-five times, but this report comes from the same source as that which recounts a long conversation between him and a Christian monk in 'the land of Rūm' which ended in the latter's conversion to Islam, and is to be treated rather as legend than as sober fact.[17] Even the date of his death is disputed, some authorities assigning it to the year 261/874 and others to 264/877.[18] The abundance of anecdotes which we owe to his devoted followers, prominent among them his nephew Abū Mūsā,[19] and the noted Sufi Aḥmad ibn Khiḍrūya[20] who met him at Mecca,[21] are more helpful to an analysis of his acts and sayings than to the construction of his biography. One series of these stories appears to be of some psychological value for the light they throw on his relations with his mother. In them we are even taken back to Abū Yazīd's pre-natal period; while his mother was pregnant with him she experienced an intuitive revulsion from any food that had the least suspicion of being ritually unclean.[22] One saying of his suggests a mother-fixation: 'Women are in a fairer state than we. A woman becomes clean once every month, and may even become clean twice in a month, for she washes herself after menstruation. We scarcely become clean once in our whole lives.'[23] On one occasion, on being asked how he had come to attain his high spiritual estate, he answered, 'You may say what you please, but my own view is that it was the result of my mother's satisfaction with me.'[24] There was a story behind this; one night, presumably when he was a boy, he was asked by his mother to bring her a drink. He went out to fetch water, and on returning found her fast asleep; he therefore stood holding the pitcher until she woke again. 'Abū Yazīd, where is the water?' his mother cried. 'Here it is!' the dutiful son responded, holding out the vessel. When his mother proposed to take it from him, she discovered that it was actually frozen to his fingers, and particles of his flesh came away on the handle of the pitcher. She enquired how this had come about, and he explained that he was afraid, if he set the pitcher down and fell asleep, that she would not see the water when she wanted it. 'Moreover,' he added, 'you had not ordered me to put it down, so I held on to it seeking to please you and obey your orders.' 'God be well pleased with you,' his mother exclaimed.[25]

Another anecdote with a charmingly human touch makes Abū Yazīd ask his mother if she knew of anything that had happened to him before he was fully conscious which might be the reason for his occasional failure to enjoy his devotions. She considered the matter carefully, and all that she could think of was that one time, when he was crying, she ran into a neighbour's house and gave him to lick a 'finger' of their *kāmakh*—a kind of savoury spread. 'So now strive to make amends for that!' she ended.[26] Abū Yazīd remembered two occasions on which he disobeyed his mother, and both times his wilfulness brought disaster upon him. Once he was throwing down sticks from the roof of his home; his mother called to him to stop, but he went on to throw another piece. Then remorse overcame him, and he bent over the edge of the roof to catch the stick before it reached the ground, but instead he tumbled off himself and injured his nose. Another time his mother asked him to draw water, giving him strict instructions only to carry one water-pot; instead—how like a naughty boy!—he took two pots, and no sooner was he out of the house when a drunken man came along and started knocking him about, and the vessels were broken. Both misfortunes he attributed to filial disobedience.[27] What gives especial point to these trifling anecdotes is that we have no corresponding stories about al-Bisṭāmī's relations with his father.

Much of the traditional legend naturally features instances of Abū Yazīd's exceptional austerity, and his miraculous powers. He appears to have been positively obsessed with the idea of ritual purity, to judge by one of his more arresting sayings. Asked how he started his career as an ascetic, he replied, 'God guided me to be a sower, and I sowed in my soul all kinds of devotion. Then He directed me to be a fuller, and I have kept on washing with all manner of detergents and every sort of water, but I don't think my soul is cleansed yet.'[28] Abū Mūsā al-Dabīlī[29] related how he visited al-Bisṭāmī one day and found him with a pool of water shimmering before him. The saint explained that a man had come and asked him what shame meant, and he discoursed to him for some time on that topic, whereupon his questioner had suddenly spun round in a circle and turned into the pool there on the floor.[30] Flying was for him a commonplace occurrence, and he had a profound explanation for it and similar occult phenomena. 'When a man's soul finds delight in his heart, and his heart rejoices in his good thoughts about his Lord, and his thoughts are pure in his desire, and his desire is united with the will of his Creator, then he wills with God's will, he sees in accord with God, his heart mounts up with God's sublimity, and his soul is moved by God's omnipotence. Such a man then journeys wherever he wills with God's will, and alights wherever he wills, God's knowledge and omnipotence being in every place. He is with God in every place, and no place is void of him; for being with God, no place is void of him, whereas if he were not with God he would not be in any place. The man's soul is united with his heart, his heart with his thoughts, his thoughts with his desire, and his desire with the will of God. God says, "I am with My servant's thoughts of Me"; so if God is with His servant's thoughts whenever he thinks, it is as though the servant is wherever God is, and just as God is never privy from the servant wherever he may be, so the servant is never privy from God wherever God may be; and God is never privy from any place to the exclusion of any place. If the servant's good thoughts of God are pure, then his thoughts fall in with God, his heart with his thoughts, and his soul with his heart, so that he travels from wherever he wills to wherever he wills by the will of God, and everything comes to him where he is without any effort on his part. All the east and the west comes to him, and whatever place he thinks of, that place attends on him, not he on the place; for he passes not away at all, being as he is with Him who exists from eternity to eternity, so that he is himself He who exists from eternity to eternity. So understand that; things follow him, not he things, all things being of God.'[31]

This very revealing statement, which is quoted on the good authority of Abū Mūsā al-Dabīlī, is of great importance for its bearing on the most famous of Abū Yazīd's miracles, his celebrated *mi'rāj* or spiritual ascension. Numerous versions of this incident are given in the hagiologies; one treatise, incorrectly attributed to al-Junaid the eminent Baghdad mystic (d. 298/910) but in fact the work of a much more obscure writer of the 8/14th century,[32] gives a particularly full account of the wonder.[33] The theme was indeed a favourite one among the Sufis; al-Qushairī (d. 465/1072), the author of the best-known general treatise on Moslem mysticism, has left a monograph in which he collected together all the material on the topic at his disposal.[34] The inspiration for these essays into the spiritual heights was provided by the accounts given by traditionists of the Prophet Mohammed's marvellous night-journey.[35] The scriptural sanction for the legend is the laconic statement in Koran XVII 1:

Glory be to Him, who carried His servant by night
from the Holy Mosque to the Further Mosque
the precincts of which We have blessed,
that We might show him some of Our signs.

This highly suggestive text was thought to be further elaborated by Koran LIII 4–17:

This is naught but a revelation revealed,
taught him by one terrible in power,
very strong; he stood poised,
being on the higher horizon,
then drew near and suspended hung,
two bows'-length away, or nearer,
then revealed to his servant that he revealed.
His heart lies not of what he saw;
what, will you dispute with him what he sees?
Indeed, he saw him another time
by the Lote-Tree of the Boundary
nigh which is the Garden of the Refuge,
when there covered the Lote-Tree that which covered;
his eye swerved not, nor swept astray.
Indeed, he saw one of the greatest signs of his Lord.

The conventional explanation of this passage is that it refers to Mohammed's vision of Gabriel; the bolder Sufis, among them evidently al-Bisṭāmī, understood it as being an obscure hint of a vision of God.[36] One of Abū Yazid's descriptions of such an experience in his own case runs as follows. 'Once He raised me up and stationed me before Him and said to me, "Abū Yazīd, My creatures desire to see thee." I said, "Adorn me in Thy uniqueness, and clothe me in Thy selfhood, and raise me up to Thy oneness, so that when Thy creatures see me they may say, We have seen thee, and Thou wilt be that, and I shall not be here." '[37] This saying, like other dark utterances of Abū Yazīd's, was later commented on by al-Junaid, the paragon of the 'sober' Sufis, who explained the striking concluding phrase by citing the Tradition, so beloved by the mystics, according to which God said to the Prophet, 'My servant continues to draw near to Me by acts of supererogation until I love him;

and when I love him, I am his eye by which he sees, his ear by which he hears, his tongue by which he speaks, and his band by which he grasps.'[38]

His first adventure into mystical union is reported by al-Bisṭāmī thus. 'The first time I travelled to His uniqueness I became a bird whose body was of oneness, and its wings of everlastingness. I continued to fly in the air of howness ten years, until I had travelled to the like air a hundred thousand times. I went on flying, until I reached the arena of pre-eternity and there beheld the tree of oneness.' He then described its soil, its trunk, branch, twigs and fruit, concluding, 'I gazed at it, and realised that all this is a deception.'[39] In another narrative the familiar mystical image of plunging into the sea[40] is substituted for that of flight: 'I vanished into almightiness, and forded the seas of dominion and the veils of godhead, until I came to the Throne; and behold, it was empty. So I cast myself upon it, saying, "Master, where shall I seek Thee?" Then He unveiled, and I saw that I was I, and I was I, turning back into what I sought, and I myself, not other than I, was where I was going.'[41] The same apprehension of identity with God runs through many of Abū Yazīd's sayings. 'When He brought me to the brink of the Divine Unity,' he once remarked, 'I divorced myself and betook myself to my Lord, calling upon Him to succour me. "Master," I cried, "I beseech Thee as one to whom nothing else remains." When He recognised the sincerity of my prayer, and how I had despaired of myself, the first token that came to me proving that He had answered this prayer was that He caused me to forget myself utterly, and to forget all creatures and all dominions. So I was stripped of all cares, and remained without any care. Then I went on traversing one kingdom after another; whenever I came to them I said to them, "Stand, and let me pass." So I would make them stand, and I would pass until I reached them all. So He drew me near, appointing for me a way to Him nearer than soul to body. Then He said, "Abū Yazīd, all of them are My creatures, except thee." I replied, "So I am Thou, and Thou art I, and I am Thou." '[42]

Confronted by such a wealth of narratives of this kind, it seems unreasonable to doubt that Abū Yazīd really passed through experiences in which he felt himself to be at one with God. It is true that there are phrases, not surprisingly, which betray a meditation of the Koran; for instance, the expression 'appointing for me a way to Him nearer than soul to body' recalls the famous context Koran L 15:

> We indeed created man; and We know what his soul whispers within him, and We are nearer to him than the jugular vein.

It is also true that these sayings abound in technical terms—such words as *waḥdānīya*, *aḥadīya*, *anānīya*, *huwīya*, *laisīya*, *daimūmīya*, *malakūt*, *jabarūt*, *lāhūt*—which suggest that al-Bisṭāmī was using an established mystical vocabulary rather than that he himself created it; and this raises problems of provenance which are probably insoluble, for we know all too little about his theosophical background and formation. But in studying his utterances one gathers the strong impression, not created by any means by all Sufi pronouncements, that he was a man who spoke of things which he had known personally and did not weave a pattern of words for effect's sake.[43]

It was this overpowering sensation of being rapt into the Godhead that caused him to utter such blasphemies, so detestable to the orthodox, as his notorious *Subḥānī! Mā a'ẓama sha'nī!* ('Glory be to Me! How great is My majesty!')[44] This saying troubled even al-Junaid, who discussed its meaning with Ibn Sālim (d. 297/910)[45] at Basra.[46] Ibn Sālim condemned it as being even more monstrous than Pharaoh's boast in Koran LXXIX 24:

> 'I am your Lord, the Most High!'

Pharaoh's use of the term 'Lord' could be explained as being no more offensive than its employment in such common expressions as 'So-and-so is *rabbu dārin*, or *rabbu mālin*, or *rabbu baitin*' ('lord of a dwelling, wealth, a house'); but there was no mitigating the horrid significance of what Abū Yazīd had said. To this al-Junaid replied that if al-Bisṭāmī did in fact utter this expression—and he had made a journey to Bistam purposely to investigate the report, to find that Abū Yazīd's own household had no knowledge of it—the matter could still be quite easily disposed of. If one overheard a man saying

There is no god but I; so serve Me

one would not make the mistake of supposing that he was being blasphemous; obviously he was merely reciting Koran XXI 25.[47] In the same way Abū Yazīd in crying 'Glory be to Me' was simply reporting God, not referring to himself. But this construction is altogether too ingenuous. Let us consider a few more of his sayings. A man one day knocked at his door; Abū Yazīd called, 'Whom do you want?' The man replied, 'Abū Yazīd.' Abū Yazīd retorted, 'Pass on; there is no one in the house but God.'[48] On another occasion a man recited in his presence Koran LXXXV 12:

Surely thy Lord's assault is terrible.

Abū Yazīd remarked, 'By His life, my assault is more terrible than His assault.'[49] A man asked him, 'How are you this morning?' He answered, 'There is no morning and no evening. Morning and evening only apply to him who is seized by attribute, and I have no attribute.'[50] One utterance bears the very hall-mark of ecstatic rapture: *Anā lā anā anā anā li-annī anā huwa anā huwa anā huwa huwa* ('I am not I I I because I am He I am He I am He He').[51] Another saying is noteworthy as anticipating the famous *Anā 'l-Ḥaqq*

('I am the Truth') which cost al-Ḥallāj (d. 309/922) his life: 'There is no truth but I am it.'[52] But the most convincing evidence of al-Bisṭāmī's claim to have become identified with God is given in a long report which we owe to Abū Mūsā al-Dabīlī; it is Abū Yazīd speaking.[53]

'I gazed upon My Lord with the eye of certainty,[54] after He had turned me away from other than Him and had illumined me with His light; and He showed me marvellous things of His secret. He also showed me His Selfhood, and I gazed upon my identity with His Selfhood; and there passed away my light in His Light, my glory in His Glory, my power in His Power. I saw my identity with His Selfhood, my honour with His Honour, my exaltation with His Exaltation. Then I gazed upon Him with the eye of truth, and said to Him, "Who is this?" He said, "This is neither I nor other than I. There is no god but I." Then He changed me out of my identity into His Selfhood, and caused me to pass away from my selfhood through His Selfhood, showing me His Selfhood uniquely; and I gazed upon Him with His Selfhood. So, when I gazed upon the Truth through the Truth, I saw the Truth through the Truth; and I continued in the Truth through the Truth for a time, having neither breath, nor tongue, nor ear, nor any knowledge; until God created for me a knowledge out of His Knowledge, and a tongue out of His Grace, and an eye out of His Light. Then I gazed upon Him with His Light, and knew Him through His Knowledge, and communed with Him with the tongue of His Grace, saying, "How fares it with me with Thee?" He said, "I am thine through thee; there is no god but thou." I said, "Delude me not through me; I choose not me instead of Thee apart from Thee, that I should choose Thee instead of Thee apart from me." Then He bestowed upon me Him instead of me, and I communed with Him through Him instead of me; and I said, "What have I from Thy hand as coming from Thee, O my Desire?" He said, "Take My commandment and My forbidding." I said, "And what have I of Thy commandment and Thy forbidding?" He said, "My praising thee in respect of My commandment and My forbidding; I thank thee for what thou hast done of My commandment, and I love thee for what thou has eschewed of My forbidding." I said, "If Thou art thankful, bestow the thanks for it upon Thyself; but if Thou blamest, Thou art not the proper object of blame, O Thou my Desire, and my Hope in my suffering, and my Cure in my misery. Thou are the One commanding, and Thou are the One commanded; there is no god but Thou."

'Then He was silent towards me, and I knew that His silence was a sign of His good pleasure. Then He said, "Who made thee to know?" I said, "He that asks knows better than he who is asked. Thou art the Answerer, and Thou art the Answered. Thou art the Asker, and Thou art the Asked. There is no god but Thou." God's proof to me through Him thus ended, and I was well pleased with Him through Him, and He was well pleased with me through Him; for I existed through Him, and He was He, and there was no god but He. Then He lit me with the light of the Essence, and I gazed upon him with the eye of Divine Bounty; and He said, "Ask what thou wilt of My Bounty, and I will give it thee." I said, "Thou art more bountiful than Thy Bounty; Thou art more generous than Thy Generosity. I am content with Thee in Thee, and I have come in the end to Thee. Offer not to me other than Thee, and repel me not from Thee with aught instead of Thee. Delude me not with Thy Grace, Thy Generosity or Thy Bounty. For Bounty is of Thee evermore, and unto Thee it returns. Thou art the Returner, and Thou art the Returned; Thou art the Seeker, and Thou art the Sought. Desire is cut off from Thee, and asking is cut off from Thee through Thee." Then He did not answer me for a time; but presently He answered me, saying, "Truth it is that thou has spoken, truth thou hast heard, truth thou hast seen, truth thou hast confirmed." I said, "Yes indeed; Thou art the Truth, and through the Truth the Truth is seen. Thou art the Truth, and through the Truth the Truth is confirmed. Thou art the Truth, and through the Truth the Truth is heard. Thou art the Hearer, and the One who gives to hear. Thou art the Truth, and the One who makes true. There is no god except Thee." He said, "Thou art naught but the Truth, and the truth thou hast spoken." I said, "Rather, Thou art the Truth, and Thy words are true, and the Truth through Thee is true. Thou art Thou; there is no god except Thee." Then He said to me, "What art thou?" I said to Him, "What art Thou?" He said, "I am the Truth." I said, "I am through Thee." He said, "If thou art through Me, then I am thou and thou art I." I said, "Delude me not with Thee instead of Thee. No indeed; Thou art Thou; there is no god except Thee."

'So when I had reached unto the Truth, and stood with the Truth through the Truth, He created for me the wing of glory and majesty; and I flew with my wing, yet I did not attain to the extremity of His Glory and Majesty. So I called upon Him, beseeching Him to succour me against Him, for I had no power against Him save in Him. Then He gazed upon me with the eye of munificence, and strengthened me with His Strength; and He adorned me, and crowned me with the crown of His Generosity upon my head. He made me unique in His Uniqueness, and one in His Oneness; and He attributed me with His Attributes, the which none shares with Him. Then He said, "Become single in My Singularity, and unique in My Uniqueness. Lift up thy head with the crown of My Generosity, and be glorious in My Glory, and majestic in My Majesty. Go forth with My Attributes unto My creatures, that I may see My Selfhood in thy selfhood. Whosoever sees thee, will see Me; and whosoever seeks thee, will seek Me, O thou My light in My earth, and My ornament in My heaven." But I said, "Thou art my seeing in mine eye, and my knowledge in my ignorance. Be Thou Thy Light, that Thou mayest be seen through Thee. There is no god but Thou." Then He answered me with the tongue of good pleasure, saying, "How well thou knowest, O My servant!" I said, "Thou art the Knower, and Thou art the Known; Thou art the Singler, and Thou art the Single. Be single in Thy Singularity, and unique in Thy Uniqueness; and do not preoccupy me with Thee, to the exclusion of Thee." God's proof to me in His Singularity thus ended, and through His Uniqueness in His Uniqueness; and I abode with Him in His Singularity, without my being singled, so that I abode with Him through Him. My attributes passed away through His Attributes, my name failed in His Name, my primality failed in His Primality, and my ultimity failed in His Ultimity.

'Then I gazed at Him through His Essence, that the qualifiers see not, the knowers attain not, and the labourers understand not; while He gazed at me with the eye of His Essence, after there had failed my name, my qualities, my first, my last, and my description. Then He called me by His Name, and addressed me by His Selfhood, and communed with me by His Oneness, saying, "O I!" I said, "O Thou!" Then He said to me, "O thou!" God's proof to me by Himself thus ended; not a Name of His Names did He name me by, without I named Him by the same, and not a Quality of His Qualities did He qualify me by, without I qualified Him by the same. So everything was cut off from me through Him; and I continued for an age without spirit or body, as one dead. Then He revived me with my life, after that He had mortified me, saying, "Whose is the Kingdom to-day?" I said, when He revived me, "God's, the One, the Omnipotent."[65] He said, "Whose is the Name?" I said, "God's, the One, the Omnipotent." He said, "Whose is the Rule to-day?" I said, "God's, the One, the Omnipotent." He said, "Whose is the Choice?" I said, "The Lord's, the All-compeller." He said, "I have revived thee with *My* Life, and made thee king over My Kingdom, and named thee by My Name, and given thee to rule with My Rule, and made thee to understand My Choice, and matched thee with the Names of Lordship and the Qualities Everlasting." I said, "I know not what Thou desirest. I belonged to myself, yet Thou approvedst not; and I belonged to Thee through Thee, yet Thou approvedst not." He said, "Belong not either to thyself or to Me. I was thine when thou wast not, so be thou Mine when thou art not; and be thine when thou art, and be Mine when thou art." I said, "How can I do that, except through Thee?"

'Then He gazed upon me with the eye of Power, and naughted me through His Being, and manifested in me through His Essence; and I existed through Him. The communing thus ended, and the word became one, and the All became one through the All. Then He said to me, "O thou!" And I said through Him, "O I!" Then He said to me, "Thou art the single." I said, "I am the single." He said to me, "Thou art thou." I said, "I am I. If I had been I in respect of I, I would not have said I; so since I was never I, be Thou Thou!" He said, "I am I." My speaking of His Identity was like in Unity to my speaking of His Selfhood. So my qualities became the Qualities of Lordship, and my tongue the Tongue of Unity, and my qualities were "He is He, there is no god but He." Whatever was, it was through His Being that it was, and whatever would be, through His Being it would be. My qualities were the Qualities of Lordship, my references the References of Everlastingness, my tongue the Tongue of Unity.'[56]

This long text, which has only recently become available, is of capital importance not only as a singularly interesting description of what was clearly a genuine experience, but also in its bearing on the later development of Sufi doctrine. Here, as so often, al-Bisṭāmī was striving to give expression to his awareness of the annihilation of the subject-object relationship in the supreme mystical encounter; but he also seems to adumbrate a theory which afterwards acquired great value, the theory of the pre-eternal compact between God and man and its honouring in the mystic's interior life. The crucial words are the passage, 'I was thine when thou wast not, so be thou Mine when thou art not.' It was al-Junaid who first formulated this idea distinctly, but it does not appear unreasonable to conjecture that he drew his inspiration from studying and expounding the ecstatic utterances of his Persian predecessor.

The constant preoccupation of al-Junaid was with interpreting the Moslem dogma of *tauḥid*—belief in the Divine Unity—in terms of mystical experience. *Tauḥid* had engaged the acute attention of the Mu'tazila, the 'People of Justice and the Divine Unity,' and their study of the problem had led them to deny attributes to God.[57] The Sufis, seeking to accommodate their spiritual discovery to theological doctrine, now took the step of proposing—to use al-Junaid's famous phrase—'the separation of the Eternal from that which was originated in time.'[58] A modern Moslem scholar, Dr. Ali Abdul Kader, has explained al-Junaid's pregnant definition as implying (1) to separate the *Eternal Essence* from the originated essence, i.e. to fix oneself or hold fast to this Essence of God and to disprove or reject all others; (2) to separate the *Attributes* contained therein from all other attributes, i.e. to fix, or hold fast to, the Attributes of God, and to disprove or refute all others; (3) to separate *Actions*, i.e. to separate the Actions of God and to disprove and refute all others. 'All of these,' he goes on, 'His Attributes and His Actions, are so completely absorbed in His Essence that he who is in the state to comprehend this Unification sees that Essence, Attributes, and Actions are all completely absorbed in the Essence of God. He comes to this as he himself in this state is absorbed in God.'[59] Even Ibn Taimīya approved of this formula.[60] The final stage of *tauḥid* was described by al-Junaid as that mystical situation in which 'the worshipper returns to his first state, that he is as he was before he existed.'[61]

Dr. Abdul Kader sees in this notion an echo of Neoplatonic ideas, and cites Plotinus: 'Before we had our becoming here, we existed There, men other than now; we were pure souls.'[62] It may well be that Neoplatonist influence was at work in the construction of this part of Sufi theosophy; but there seems to be room for doubting whether

Plotinus' doctrine of the pre-existence of the soul, afterwards accepted by Moslem philosophers,[63] is in fact identical with the Sufi conception of man existing in God before his birth in time. The distinction is perhaps a fine one, but it is not unimportant; for al-Junaid's formulation, provoked as it may have been by al-Bisṭāmī's 'I was thine when thou wast not,' proved more readily assimilable to Islam than Avicenna's[64]

> Out of her lofty home she hath come down
> Upon thee, this white dove in all the pride
> Of her reluctant beauty.

For the Sufi doctrine had the great merit of being able to invoke scriptural sanction. Koran LXXVI 1 was thought to refer to this pre-natal naughting in God:

> Has there come on man a while of time
> when he was a thing unremembered?

But the critical text brought forward as proving an encounter with God before man's earthly existence is Koran VII 171:

> And when thy Lord took from the Children of Adam,
> from their loins, their seed, and made them testify
> touching themselves, 'Am I not your Lord?'
> They said, 'Yes, we testify.'

'In this verse,' comments al-Junaid, 'God tells you that He spoke to them at a time when they did not exist, except so far as they existed in Him. This existence is not the same type of existence as is usually attributed to God's creatures; it is a type of existence which only God knows and only He is aware of. God knows their existence; embracing them He sees them in the beginning when they are non-existent and unaware of their future existence in this world. The existence of these is timeless.'[65]

We may now realise more clearly the significance of the form of Divine colloquy in which al-Bisṭāmī expresses his experience of reabsorption into God. God spoke to man before creation; He will also speak to man on the Last Day, though sinners will not enjoy that privilege.[66] It was the unique distinction of Moses, among the Prophets, to hear God's voice, as we learn from Koran IV 162:

> And unto Moses God spoke directly.

The legend of Mohammed's Night Journey has him converse with God in the seventh heaven.[67] The mystic in his spiritual Ascension was at once re-enacting the scene in which man entered into his primeval covenant with the Creator, and anticipating the final consumation when God will speak to the saved. During his days on earth he enjoyed moments of high ecstasy that restored him to 'the stage at which I was at the beginning.'[68] It was of this experience that al-Junaid sang:[69]

> Now I have known, O Lord,
> What lies within my heart;
> In secret, from the world apart,
> My tongue hath talked with my Adored.

Later al-Niffarī (d. *ca.* 365/976)[70] and Ibn 'Arabī[71] were to make books out of their conversations with God.

The Sufis thus claimed to have proved by personal contact with the Creator those truths of the Divine Unity which the theologians and the philosophers were endeavouring laboriously to expound. But there was a further riddle to be solved—the riddle of existence itself. If God was the Self-sufficient Being that He described Himself to be,[72] what was the compelling motive that induced Him to create the world? 'Thou art the Seeker, and Thou art the Sought,' said Abū Yazīd to God in the course of his long conversation. In another bold saying he states, 'Moses desired to see

God.[73] I did not desire to see God; God desired to see me.'[74] Elsewhere he tells us that the ecstatic mystic is 'like a mirror with six faces; when God desires to look upon His creation, He looks upon this man who is His mirror and sees in him His creation, and orders their affairs.'[75] A famous Tradition, perennially popular with the Sufis, represents God as telling Mohammed, 'I was a hidden treasure and I desired to be known; therefore I created the creation in order that I might be known.'[76] In the scattered hints given in Abū Yazīd's reported sayings it seems legitimate to find the germs of that doctrine of the Perfect Man which was to play so large a part in later Sufi speculation. He is indeed credited with the statement that 'the perfect and complete man' is one who after having been invested with Divine attributes becomes unconscious of them; R. A. Nicholson denies that the term as employed by al-Bisṭāmī 'bears the peculiar significance attached to it by Ibnu 'l-'Arabí and Jílí',[77] that is, of the Perfect Man as 'a microcosmic being through whom God's consciousness is manifested to Himself.'[78] But on the new evidence it looks as if Abū Yazīd in fact had some such idea in mind; and al-Ḥallāj, who must have studied his sayings attentively, may have taken a hint from them in working out his own theory of Love as the essence of God's essence. 'Before the creation God loved Himself in absolute unity and through love revealed Himself to Himself alone. Then, desiring to behold that love-in-aloneness, that love without otherness and duality, as an external object, He brought forth from non-existence an image of Himself, endowed with all His attributes and names.'[79] To al-Ḥallāj that being who held up a mirror to God was Adam; al-Bisṭāmī had already identified it with himself.

It is interesting to see how the Sufi doctrine of direct encounter with God, and of the Perfect Man, became reconciled with orthodoxy. It was perhaps fortunate for al-Bistāmī that he lived so far away from the Abbasid capital, and so escaped collision with the theologians of

Baghdad; otherwise his claim to have been told by God 'Thou art the Truth' might well have brought upon him the same fate as that which overtook al-Ḥallāj when he echoed him by saying 'I am the Truth.' But the sounder reputation of men like al-Muḥāsibī and al-Junaid, coinciding with a lessening in the theological tension after the destruction of the Mu'tazila, encouraged writers such as al-Kalābādhī[80] and al-Qushairī to argue that Sufism, with its sting drawn, so far from conflicting with the now widely accepted tenets of Ash'arī Islam, actually confirmed them. When al-Ghazālī added the weight of his authority to this irenic movement, the concordat between 'sober' Sufism and Sunnī dogmatics was assured.

Despite the celebrated account which al-Ghazālī gives of his 'conversion',[81] it is open to discussion whether he was himself a mystic at all in the strict sense of the term.[82] However that may be, to him belongs the great merit of having recognised spiritual experience as a valid and indeed superior proof of the existence of God. 'It is not so improbable,' he argues in one place, 'O you who inhabit the world of reason, that beyond reason there exists another plane in which appear things that do not appear in reason, just as it is not improbable that reason should be a plane transcending discrimination and sensation, in which strange and marvellous things are revealed that sensation and discrimination fall short of attaining.'[83] The faculty to which he refers is intuition, possessed in a superlative degree by prophets but of which saints also have a generous share.[84] Elsewhere al-Ghazālī elaborates this point in terms that clearly hark back to what al-Kindī and al-Fārābī had propounded.[85] He has been discussing the varieties of human knowledge, and reaches finally the knowledge of intelligibles which is attained 'either by Divine inspiration, or by learning and acquisition. Such knowledge supervenes either swiftly or slowly, and there is a difference between the ranks of scientists, philosophers, saints and prophets in respect of it. . . . The furthest reach is the degree of the prophet, to whom all or most realities are revealed without conscious acquisition or effort, but rather by Divine revelation, in the swiftest possible time. This is the happiness (*sa'āda*) which comes upon a man and brings him near to God, such nearness not being local or spatial but spiritual and real. Courtesy demands the firm holding of the reins of expression in this station; for some have gone so far as to claim unification, beyond nearness. One said, "Glory be to me! How great is my majesty!" Another said, "I am the Truth." Another expressed the idea of "indwelling"; while the Christians have declared the unification of Godhead and manhood, saying of Jesus that he is one-half of God.'[86]

In another context al-Ghazālī reproduces the advice he received from a leading Sufi when he first resolved to follow the mystical path. 'The way,' his spiritual director told him, 'is to cut off entirely your connexions with the world, so that your heart no longer pays attention to family or children, wealth or homeland, learning or sainthood; rather you reach a state in which it is the same to you whether these things exist or not. Then you retire by yourself into a corner, confining yourself in your devotions to the prescribed religious duties and offices. There you sit with your heart unpreoccupied and purpose concentrated, turning your recollection upon God. In the first stage you assiduously apply your tongue to the mention of God, saying incessantly Allah Allah, your heart being present and conscious. In time you reach a state in which, even if you gave up moving your tongue, you would as it were see the word flowing over your tongue by sheer force of habit. Then you continue with the same application until the impression of the tongue is effaced, and you discover your soul and your heart to be persevering in this recollection without the tongue moving at all. You go on like that, and presently nothing remains in your heart but the meaning of the word; the letters of pronunciation and the shape of the word do not impinge any more on your mind, only the meaning, quite detached, continues present in your heart, cleaving to it uninterruptedly. Choice is yours only as far as this point; after that you have no choice left, except to seek to continue to repel diverting temptations. Then your choice is cut off altogether, and nothing remains for you but to wait for such disclosures as may manifest themselves, like those which have appeared to the saints, being part of what appears to the prophets. It may be something like a sudden flash of lightning which does not persist; then it returns, it may be after a long while. If it does return, it may either persist or be snatched away again; if it persists, it may do so for a long or a short time. Similar flashes may occur successively, so to speak supporting one another; or it may not be confined to a single variety. The stages of God's saints are innumerable, according to the wide differences in their natures and characters.'[87]

The author remarks that the validity of the Sufi method is indisputable; undeniably it brings those who practise it to their goal, which is the sublime state enjoyed by saints and prophets. But this kind of discipline is not without serious dangers; the reason may be affected, the health of the body may be destroyed, and melancholy may ensue. 'If the soul has not been exercised in the sciences that deal with fact and demonstration, it will acquire mental phantasms that it will suppose to be truths descending upon it. Many a Sufi has continued for ten years in one such fancy before escaping from it, whereas if he had had a sound scientific education he would have been delivered out of it at once.'[88] From this we may conclude that intuition, the fruits of ascetic discipline, is accepted in the Ghazalian system as providing a conclusive confirmation of the truths of revelation, but it must always be rooted in and remain under the control of trained reason. 'The best course is for a man first to follow the path of scientific study, and to acquire by laborious learning as much of the demonstrative sciences as human power can encompass.... After that there is no harm in his electing to withdraw from the world and to devote himself entirely to God in an expectant mood; it may well be that things will be revealed to him by this method of which the followers of the Sufi path alone have received but confused impressions. That at least is what I think,' al-Ghazālī concludes. 'The true knowledge rests with God.'[89]

A further reconciliation of Sufi theosophy with orthodox Islam was effected by the promulgation of the theory that the pre-eternal essence of Mohammed (*al-ḥaqīqat al-Muḥammadīya*) was identical with what the philosophers called the First Intelligence,[90] 'the medium through which God becomes conscious of Himself in creation.'[91] This fruitful speculation was worked out most fully by al-Jīlī (d. 832/1428) in his celebrated monograph *The Perfect Man*,[92] but it was already incorporated by Ibn 'Arabī into his all-embracing system,[93] and was given emotional—as distinct from intellectual—value in the poetry of Ibn al-Fāriḍ (d. 632/1235). If unification with God Himself was too blasphemous a notion to be given permanent lodging in the house of Islam, less objection could obviously be taken to the proposal that the mystic's quest was unification with the essence of Mohammed. A convenient Tradition had been discovered proclaiming that Mohammed had been a prophet while Adam was still 'between clay and water';[94] it was therefore with the essence of Mohammed that God had spoken on the day of the primeval covenant. In becoming a perfect man, the Sufi automatically achieved union with the Perfect Man. The beginnings of the mystical cult of Mohammed are traceable back at least as far as al-Ḥallāj, whose hymn to the Prophet served as a model to later enthusiasts: 'All the Lights of the Prophets proceeded from his Light; he was before all, his name the first in the Book of Fate; he was known before all things and all being, and will endure after the end of all. By his guidance have all eyes attained to sight. . . . All knowledge is a drop from his ocean, all wisdom a handful from his stream, all times an hour from his life.'[95] So Ibn al-Fāriḍ, whose odes contain many passages where the pilgrimage to Mecca is interpreted as an encounter with a spiritual beloved,[96] in his great

Poem of the Way celebrates his unification with the Spirit of Mohammed in language that reveals his conviction of identification with the perfect image of God who 'encompasses all things with his knowledge, power and glory.'[97] Abū Yazīd's error in supposing himself superior to the founder of Islam[98] was thus triumphantly corrected; his claim to be himself God's mirror was translated into the more acceptable thesis of being one with God's mirror. Using the first person to make clear beyond all doubt his transformation into the eternal essence of Mohammed, Ibn al-Fāriḍ makes bold to assert:[99]

I am not blameworthy, if I proclaim
My gifts, and on my followers bestow
My grand endowment: that dispenser of
The mystic union, when he greeted me
At *Yea or nearer*, pointed me a bond
Of spiritual kinship. From his light
The lantern of my essence shone on me;
My eve in me was radiant as my morn. . . .
My moon set not; my sun ne'er sank from sight;
By me are guided all the shining stars
Upon their courses; all the planets swim
About my heavens as my will controls
All things I own; my angels prostrate fall
Before my sovereignty. And in the world
Of recollection still the soul doth own
Its ancient knowledge my disciples pray
That I bestow on them. Haste then to my
Eternal union, wherein I have found
The greybeards of the tribe as little babes!

Ibn al-Fāriḍ did not however escape from the charge of pantheism which was preferred, and more deservedly so, against his Andalusian contemporary Ibn 'Arabī. Theo-logian critics, who continued even after al-Ghazālī to regard Sufism with deep suspicion, were never slow to fasten on to ambiguous phrases in the writings of the mystics as proving them guilty of the 'incarnationist' heresy. Jalāl al-Dīn Rūmī (d. 672/1273) might explain away the hateful *Anā 'l-Ḥaqq* of al-Ḥallāj with consummate ingenuity,[100] and offer an equally plausible interpretation for al-Bisṭāmī's scandalous *Subḥānī*.[101] But Ibn al-Jauzī (d. 597/1200), that tireless Ḥanbalī polygraph, had already declared war on all ecstatic utterances in his *Devil's Delusion*;[102] with Ibn 'Arabī's massive output now presenting a mammoth target for the arrows of enraged orthodoxy, added to the fresh memory of Yaḥyā al-Suhrawardī's execution at Aleppo,[103] Ibn Taimīya of Damascus found ample scope for the display of his polemical acumen in attacking the theosophical excesses of the Sufis. Pouring scorn on the doctrine of the Unity of Being (*waḥdat al-wujūd*) and its corollary that only God existed,[104] he quoted with huge glee the retort made by a simple believer to a Sufi of the Ibn 'Arabī school who told him that anyone declaring anything but God to exist was a liar: 'Then who is it that told the lie?'[105] The fantastic sayings recorded of Abū Yazīd al-Bisṭāmī were the utterances of a spiritual drunkard; as for the blasphemy of al-Ḥallāj, that was to be put on a par with the pretensions of Shī'ite extremists about 'Alī, or the Fāṭimid al-Ḥākim, or Christian claims regarding Jesus.[106] Ibn Taimīya even goes so far as to see in the dissemination of Sufi pantheism 'the chief cause for the emergence of the Tartars and the obliteration of the holy law of Islam; they are the advance-guard of Antichrist.'[107]

The quarrel between the theologians and the theosophists raged far and wide during the succeeding centuries, and is still not ended; the history of that last great controversy in Islam has yet to be written. India in the seventeenth century provided the scene for one particularly interesting chapter of the melancholy story. Dārā Shukoh, the eldest son of the Moghul emperor Shāh Jahān, inherited from his great-grandfather Akbar a taste for religious speculation. Early in his life he came under Sufi influence, and was moved by the spirit of tolerance inculcated by his mystical preceptors to attempt to promote a harmony between Islam and Hinduism on the basis of similarities between the teachings of Sufism and the Vedanta.[108] Had he succeeded his father on the Peacock Throne, instead of being ousted and slain by his brother Aurangzēb, the subsequent history of India might have been very different. But Aurangzēb, also called 'Ālamgīr, was a Sunnī zealot, and his accession put an end to any hope of a royally-inspired reconciliation between the two great creeds of the Moghul Empire. It was to 'Ālamgīr that Iqbāl (d. 1938), the 'spiritual founder' of Pakistan, looked back as the man[109]

> In whom Islam attained a loftier fame
> And wider honour graced the Prophet's Law,
> He the last arrow to our quiver left
> In the affray of Faith with Unbelief;
> When that the impious seed of heresy,
> By Akbar nourished, sprang and sprouted fresh
> In Dara's soul, the candle of the heart
> Was dimmed in every breast, no more secure
> Against corruption our Community
> Continued; then God chose from India
> That humble-minded warrior, Alamgir,
> Religion to revive, faith to renew.
> The lightning of his sword set all ablaze
> The harvest of impiety; faith's torch
> Once more its radiance o'er our counsels shed.

NOTES

[1] Yāqūt, *Mu'jam al-buldān* (Cairo, 1323/1906), i, p. 180.

[2] For Shapur II's building activities, see V. F. Büchner in *Encyclopaedia of Islam*, iv, pp. 315-6.

[3] For further information on Bistam, see M. Streck in *Encyclopaedia of Islam*, i, p. 733.

[4] For the biographical sources available, see al-Sulamī, *Ṭabaqāt al-Ṣūfiya*, p. 67.

[5] See al-Sahlajī, *Kitāb al-Nūr* (ed. Badawī), p. 50.

[6] See C. Brockelmann, *Geschichte der arabischen Litteratur*, Suppl., i, p. 104.

[7] *Kitāb al-Nūr*, p. 47.

[8] L. Massignon's identification of this man with al-Bisṭāmī's teacher in Traditions (see his *Essai sur les Origines*, p. 243, n. 3) is based on a misreading; the latter's name was Abū al-Raḥmān al-Suddī, see *Kitāb al-Nūr*, p. 63.

[9] See H. Ritter in *Encyclopaedia of Islam*, New Edition, i, p. 162. The source is al-Sarrāj, *Kitāb al-Luma'*, p. 177: *fa-kuntu ulaqqinuhu mā yuqīmu bihi farḍahu*. L. Massignon (*op. cit.*, *loc. cit.*) interprets this as meaning that al-Bisṭāmī taught Abū 'Alī 'droit canon (hanéfite)'!

[10] *Kitāb al-Luma'*, p. 177. The phrase is: *wa-kāna yu'allimunī t-tauḥīda wa'l-ḥaqā'iqa ṣarfan.*

[11] R. A. Nicholson, *The Mystics of Islam*, p. 17; L. Massignon, *op. cit.*, p. 80.

[12] H. Ritter in *loc. cit.*

[13] As asserted by al-Bīrūnī in his *India* (ed. Sachau), p. 43; see the discussion in L. Massignon, *op. cit.*, pp. 63-80.

[14] See al-Sam'ānī, *Kitāb al-Ansāb*, fol. 313b; Yāqūt, *op. cit.*, iii, p. 151.

[15] Yāqūt, *op. cit.*, iii, p. 152.

[16] *Kitāb al-Nūr*, p. 48.

[17] See my paper 'A Bistami Legend' in *Journal of the Royal Asiatic Society*, 1938, pp. 89–91. The text is now published in 'Abd al-Raḥmān Badawī, *Shaṭaḥāt al-Ṣūfiya*, pp. 173–6.

[18] References in al-Sulamī, *op. cit.*, *loc. cit.*

[19] See H. Ritter in *loc. cit.*

[20] See *ibid.* Aḥmad ibn Khiḍrūya also visited al-Bisṭāmī in Bistam, see *Kitāb al-Nūr*, p. 55.

[21] For further information on Aḥmad ibn Khiḍrūya, see al-Sulamī,

op. cit., pp. 103–6; Hujwiri, *Kashf al-mahjūb* (tr. R. A. Nicholson), pp. 119–21.

22 See the extract from Sibt Ibn al-Jauzi, *Mir'āt al-zamān*, printed in Badawi, *op. cit.*, p. 168.

23 *Kitāb al-Nūr*, p. 66.

24 *Ibid.*, pp. 71–2.

25 *Ibid.*, p. 71.

26 *Ibid.* For a similar childhood anecdote, see *Kitāb al-Nūr*, pp. 108–9.

27 *Ibid.*, pp. 70–1.

28 *Ibid.*, p. 66.

29 So H. Ritter (*loc. cit.*) spells the name, deriving it from Dabil in Armenia, see Yāqūt, *op. cit.*, iv, p. 36. Badawi in his edition always prints al-Daibuli (cf. Yāqūt, *op. cit.*, iv, p. 118), but this is a mistake.

30 *Kitāb al-Nūr*, p. 73.

31 *Kitāb al-Nūr*, p. 75.

32 C. Brockelmann, *op. cit.*, Suppl. ii, p. 124.

33 See R. A. Nicholson, 'An early Arabic version of the *Mi'rāj* of Abú Yazíd al-Bistámí' in *Islamica*, 1926, pp. 402–15. For a description of the *mi'rāj* experienced by a woman-disciple of al-Bistāmī, see *Kitāb al-Nūr*, p. 123.

34 *Kitāb al-Mi'rāj*, preserved in a unique copy in Bankipore, see Brockelmann, *op. cit.*, Suppl. i, p. 772.

35 See especially J. Horowitz in *Encyclopaedia of Islam*, iii, pp. 505–8.

36 See al-Kalābādhī, *Kitāb al-Ta'arruf*, pp. 20–22 for a discussion.

37 See al-Sarrāj, *op. cit.*, p. 382, and cf. Ibn al-Jauzī, *Talbis Iblīs*, p. 345.

38 See al-Sarrāj, *op. cit.*, pp. 383–4.

39 *Ibid.*, p. 384.

40 The image is particularly a favourite of Rūmī.

41 *Kitāb al-Nūr*, p. 128.

42 *Ibid.*, p. 119.

43 A good example of the latter type is provided by al-Tauḥīdī, whose book *al-Ishārāt al ilāhīya* is manifestly a mere literary compilation.

44 Reported in *Kitāb al-Nūr*, p. 111; see L. Massignon, *Essai*, p. 249.

45 See *Kitāb al-Luma'*, Introd. p. xix.

46 *Ibid.*, pp. 390–1.

47 For a story in which al-Bistāmī uses this quotation with reference to himself, see *Kitāb al-Nūr*, p. 122.

48 *Ibid.*, p. 131.

49 *Ibid.*, p. 111.

50 *Ibid.*, p. 111.

51 *Ibid.*, p. 111.

52 *Ibid.*, p. 108.
53 The text is given in *Kitāb al-Nūr*, pp. 138–141.
54 The phrase *'ain al-yaqīn* comes from Koran cii 7.
55 Koran xl 16.
56 *Kitāb al-Nūr*, p. 141.
57 See J. W. Sweetman, *Islam and Christian Theology*, ii, p. 122.
58 Quoted in al-Qushairī, *Risāla* (Cairo, 1330/1912), p. 3.
59 See *The Islamic Quarterly*, i, p. 170.
60 *Ibid.*, p. 171.
61 *Ibid.*, p. 174.
62 *Ibid.*, pp. 175–6, quoting Plotinus, *Enneads*, vi, 4. 14.
63 And therefore a point of difference between them and the theologians.
64 In his 'Poem of the Soul'; see A. J. Arberry, *Avicenna on Theology*, p. 77.
65 *The Islamic Quarterly*, i, p. 174.
66 Koran ii 169, iii 71.
67 See J. Horowitz in *Encyclopaedia of Islam*, iii, p. 507.
68 The *Islamic Quarterly*, i, p. 83.
69 See A. J. Arberry, *Sufism*, p. 59.
70 See my edition and translation of his collected writings.
71 In his *al-Isrā' ilā 'l-maqām al-asrā*.
72 As frequently in the Koran, cf. lxiv 6.
73 Cf. Koran vii 139.
74 *Kitāb al-Nūr*, p. 146.
75 *Ibid.*, p. 125.
76 See R. A. Nicholson, *The Mystics of Islam*, p. 80.
77 R. A. Nicholson, *Studies in Islamic Mysticism*, p. 77, n.2.
78 *Ibid.*, quoting Ibn 'Arabī, *Fuṣūṣ al-ḥikam*, ch. 1.
79 *Ibid.*, p. 80.
80 See *The Doctrine of the Sufis* (tr. A. J. Arberry), pp. xiii–xv.
81 In his *al-Munqidh min al-ḍalāl*, now newly translated by W. M. Watt.
82 I hope to discuss this question in a future study.
83 See *al-Jawāhir al-ghawālī* (Cairo, 1343/1924), p. 132.
84 *Ibid.*, p. 133.
85 See above, pp. 36, 40–1.
86 *Mīzān al-'amal* (Cairo, 1342/1923), p. 23.
87 *Ibid.*, p. 35.
88 *Ibid.*, p. 36.
89 *Ibid.*, p. 40.
90 See R. A. Nicholson, *Studies in Islamic Mysticism*, p. 112.
91 *Ibid.*, p. 110.

[92] For a new study of the doctrine of the Perfect Man, see 'Abd al-Raḥmān Badawī, *al-Insān al-kāmil fī 'l-Islām*.

[93] See R. A. Nicholson, *Studies in Islamic Mysticism*, pp. 149-61.

[94] *Ibid.*, p. 157.

[95] H. A. R. Gibb, *Mohammedanism*, p. 131.

[96] For an excellent study of his poems, see R. A. Nicholson, *Studies in Islamic Mysticism*, pp. 162–266.

[97] See *ibid.*, p. 195.

[98] As reported in *Kitāb al-Nūr*, p. 111.

[99] See my *Poem of the Way*, pp. 73–4.

[100] R. A. Nicholson, *Rūmī, Poet and Mystic*, p. 184.

[101] See *Mathnawī*, iv, 2102 ff.

[102] See *Talbīs Iblīs* (Cairo, 1369/1950), pp. 341–50.

[103] In 578/1191.

[104] *Majmū'at al-rasā'il wa'l-masā'il*, i, pp. 61–120.

[105] *Ibid.*, p. 104.

[106] *Ibid.*, pp. 168–9.

[107] *Ibid.*, pp. 179–80.

[108] In his *Majma' al-baḥrain*, published at Calcutta in 1929.

[109] *Mysteries of Selflessness* (tr. A. J. Arberry), p. 17.

INDEX

www.ingramcontent.com/pod-product-compliance
Ingram Content Group UK Ltd.
Pitfield, Milton Keynes, MK11 3LW, UK
UKHW021408190726
13845UKWH00028B/959

9 789366 081342